RECONCILIATION
Geopolitical Perspectives of a Black Theologian

by

Eric M. Betts

Copyright © 2022 Dr. Eric M. Betts

All rights reserved. No part of this publication may be reproduced, distributed, or transmitted in any form or by any means, including photocopying, recording, or other electronic or mechanical methods, without the prior written permission of the publisher, except in the case of brief quotations embodied in critical reviews and certain other noncommercial uses permitted by copyright law.

ISBN-978-1-951300-56-2

Liberation's Publishing LLC
West Point - Mississippi

RECONCILIATION
Geopolitical Perspectives of a Black Theologian

RECONCILIATION Geopolitical Perspectives of a Black Theologian

TABLE OF CONTENT

Preface 1

1 The Research, Its Rationale and The Problem Statements 5

2 The Underlying Fears Which Lead to Conflict 43

3 Lice, Labels, Lies 77

4 Christian Theology, Zionism, and Palestinian Humanity 91

5 The Theology of Reparations 135

6 The Urgent Need for Community and Human Commonality .. 155

Bibliography 215

Sermons and Lectures 221

FREEDOM IS NEVER FREE!

PREFACE

This work addresses the role that ecclesiology and Christian anthropology should play in fulfilling the Christological expectation of breaking down walls of racial and ethnic differences, nationalism and tribalism and reconciling the world as one human family. While the title suggests a broader scope for resolving conflict and the social harms of estrangement, this thesis does not seek to address comprehensively, the myriad causes of conflict. A much narrower focus on the role of conflict through the perspective of racial disparity is given. In this sense, this research may serve as a case study for resolving other complicated conflicts that interfere with humanity's harmonious existence.

For several centuries through the Transatlantic Slave Trade, colonialism, apartheid and militant Zionism, the cause of Christ has been misrepresented, manipulated and abused by a pseudo-Christianity centered around European cultural identity and domination. Although many of these ills have been lessened over the last half century, the aftereffects remain. European pseudo-Christianity and its tendency to dehumanize and exploit other ethnic groups and races of people continues. The ecclesiological assumption that Europeans have been divinely destined to evangelize, civilize and democratize the world for Christ is indeed antichrist at its core. Furthermore, Christianity, and/or a belief in a supreme creator existed in other lands, such as Palestine, Africa and Asia, before the arrival of European traders. These communities were not godless and barbaric as the stereotype suggests, but rather made significant educational, cultural and theological contributions to the world.

Additionally, true Christian anthropology suggests that all races, tribes and ethnic groups bear the image of God and have equal value and dignity under Christ. Most would admit this on a basic level, but the more this is explored and celebrated, the sooner a reconciled community of human familyhood can emerge. Analyzing this reality, requires that theologians examine the ways in which dignity has been denied across the centuries, and seek to correct them.

A Christian theology of love, reconciliation, and human dignity is an urgent need, in contradistinction to a theology of domination, conquest and economic Darwinism (survival of the strongest). It should also be noted that whenever this thesis challenges or criticizes Christian theologians, this is referring to the mainstream Christian Evangelical voices within the American context, who are privileged with proximity to the corridors of power. This critique does not include liberation theologians, nor church based civil rights leaders, who should be commended for their efforts.

While Eurocentric theology has created many rifts and chasms among nations and races, there is hope for the Christian message. This hope lies in the expectation that alternative voices will eventually gain a wider audience and that the younger generation of evangelicals will sympathize more closely with the issues of human rights. These alternative voices should be given close attention by mainstream Christian theologians, clergy, and political leaders. Those Christian theologians and clergy who have lived experiences within marginalized communities should be given a larger platform in the ecclesiological and political realm. They are uniquely capable of leading the world to reconciliation and reparation. However, Christian leaders and theologians who presently have seats at the tables of power, are challenged to utilize their influence to end oppression, war and conflict rather than further imperialistic goals.

One might suggest that the world's great powers, in most cases are not at war with weaker nations, or that those at the top of the social hierarchy are not at war with those at the bottom. The question may be asked, "Where is the conflict?" The absence of war through missiles, tanks and grenades does not necessarily mean that conflict is non-existent. Some would suggest that the more powerful nations are in fact extremely charitable toward the darker races and nations of the world. They may point to food charities and foreign aid. However, what the most powerful nations miss is that they are often the ones who have placed systems and structures in place that are the causes of the poverty. It is not enough to be charitable; one must also be just. The justice of God demands that the most powerful must tear down those systems they rely upon for their prosperity which create the impoverished conditions to begin with. This thesis advances the perspective that colonization, exploitation, xenophobia, police brutality and generational theft are as equally destructive, hostile and adversarial in nature toward vulnerable population groups as strategic warfare. Disregard for human life and dignity to further the aims of the powerful is tantamount to being victimized militarily. For example, children going hungry due to economic exploitation, or developing life-altering disease through lead poisoned water due to discrimination has the same impact as violence being committed against them. One of the fathers of black theology, Professor J. Deotis Roberts, explained this concept in the most eloquent way. He said the following:

> *Violence takes more than one form. There is covert violence as well as overt violence. Blacks suffer from both forms of violence. Covert violence is subtle and insidious. Whites often participate in this form of violence without knowing it. If they do not participate in it to a great extent, they permit it to happen without using their influence to end it. The treatment of persons as things is a form of violence.* (Roberts 1994: 100)

The Palestinian and Israeli conflict, and a militarized police state in the U.S., would be a literal example of how overt militarism is indeed exercised in these cases. These experiences have become a counterproductive hindrance to social harmony and the overall advancement of the wider community. There are many challenges facing the globe and humanity. It is extremely urgent that a theology of reconciliation be advanced for the good of all.

Key Words: familyhood, reconciliation, anthropological, eschatological, Christological, Eurocentric, colonialism, Zionism, reparations, Israelology, reparations, restorative justice, colonialism, displacement, dehumanization, generational theft,

Acronyms: ADOS (American Descendants of Slaves) and TRC (Truth and Reconciliation Commission)

Updated Language: Sources from the works of Dr. Martin Luther King Jr uses the word "brotherhood" with the intent of being inclusive, but this thesis replaces the word "brotherhood" with the more appropriate and gender-inclusive word "familyhood" and "man" with humanity or human beings.

1 THE RESEARCH, ITS RATIONALE AND THE PROBLEM STATEMENTS

1.1 Introduction

The primary theses in this research will demonstrate why political, religious, tribal, and international conflict poses a major threat to the globe we call home. There are many areas of conflict that might be explored, but lessons from the racial legacy of America, the Rwandan genocide and Palestinian occupation will be the center of attention in this thesis. The question may be asked, "Why does the writer focus on these three areas when there are so many other problem areas in the world?" Firstly, there is much that the reader can gain by understanding the lived experience in the American context; this is the catalyst and perspective that causes the writer to see more clearly problem of conflict in other lands. Secondly, the lived experience of anti-black conflict domestically opens one's eyes to see it more distinctly on a global scale. Most politically active black Americans are somewhat Afrocentric in their foreign perspective when it comes to justice and equality. Consequently, Rwanda stands out as the greatest Anti-black foreign policy failure and atrocity in the lifetime of the writer.

The South African liberation struggle is mentioned for the same reasons. Witnessing South Africans struggle for freedom on the television reminded the writer of the civil rights movement of the 1950's and 60's. Palestine is given a great amount of attention as they continue to struggle for freedom decades beyond the freedom struggles in America and South Africa. Their struggle continues in this modern age, to a great extent because of the theological support for the Israeli occupation, whereas there was little theological support for the struggles in the U.S. and South Africa. Why would a black American with an Afrocentric view of foreign affairs focus on the Palestinian plight? Michael R. Fischback, Professor of History at Randolph-Macon College explains that "Free Palestine" political expressions have historically existed among black power activists in America.

Fischbach points out that his is due to its proximity to Africa and the fact that these are a people of color who are struggling against Western domination, racism and imperialism. Additionally, he eloquently reminds his readers in his scholarly book *Black Power and Palestine* that Martin Luther King Jr., Malcolm X and Jesse Jackson had historically supported the cause of the Palestinians. Fishbach expostulates that the Black power advocates of the 1960's were the first outside of anti-war activists, to announce their solidarity with Palestinian cause and their strong opposition to Israeli occupation. He also educates his readers that black militants viewed their struggle and the Palestinian struggle as the same effort to defeat imperialism in the world. He further adds the following insight concerning black power and its connection to Palestinian solidarity:

> *Black militants latched onto the Palestinian cause as another liberation struggle waged by a people of color deserving their support. They saw themselves and the Palestinians as kindred peoples of color waging a revolution against a global system of oppression...The Palestinians were not the only Third world guerrillas they supported, but Palestine's proximity to Africa...served to make the Palestinians' cause near and dear to the hearts of many Black power advocates. (Fischbach 2019: 11-12)*

While a significant proportion of black power activists were critical of Christian churches and institutions, many viewed their political rhetoric as consistent with biblical themes of justice for the exploited, self-determination for all peoples, liberation of the oppressed and human dignity. These themes led to many Christian leaders to stand in solidarity with black power activists in their pro-Palestinian positions, world renown Christian professor and activist Cornel West of Union Theological Seminary being chief among them. While it is unclear whether the pro-Palestinian position is held by most American blacks, it is certainly a part of the black tradition of protest. In fact, National Public Radio aired a segment highlighting the support of the Palestinian struggle within the Black Lives Matter movement. Historian Robin Kelley of UCLA and his project are mentioned in the piece.

> *Delegations of Black activists, including Kelley, have visited the West Bank to see how Palestinians are living. Kelley also appeared in a video released in 2015 by activist groups, such as the Dream Defenders, Black Youth Project 100 and the Institute for Middle East Understanding, to highlight Black-Palestinian solidarity. 'When I see them, I see us,' the video's multiple narrators repeated, comparing the Palestinian struggle to the fight against police brutality in the U.S... social media images and video of last month's war [June 2020] between Israel and Hamas brought many Black Lives Matter activists in the U.S. to the streets, including Nee Nee Taylor, who attended a rally last month outside Israel's embassy in Washington, D.C. 'Palestine's struggle is our struggle... [was the theme' (Wang, 2021).]*

This explains why a black American theologian and author might focus significant attention on the Palestinian liberation struggle. It should also be noted that there is a professional and political connection between the Israeli security forces and the militarized police force in the US which profile black citizens. According to Domenica Ghanem, a pro-Palestinian and pro-Black lives activist and writer, Israeli security officers have formally engaged in training U.S. police; Chicago, Baltimore and St. Louis police forces are a few examples. This is the reason why similar tactics, such as the chokehold, are utilized by both. Both are given equipment by the U.S. military. *While the joint forces of the Israeli military and the U.S. police are a terrifying and oftentimes deadly affront, a joint Black and Palestinian force for good is emerging as quite powerful itself. And as the death toll rises here and in Gaza, it's needed now more than ever* (Ghanem 2018). When viewing all ethnic groups as a part of the Creator's divine program, all Christian theologians should be pro-Palestinian in their positions. Between the Palestinian liberation struggle and the solidarity with which the black liberation movement has stood with them, to a certain degree they may be included in the socio-economic spectrum with black people. They may be seen as existing as politically black people from the perspective of dark-skinned people struggling to exist as the liberated and fully functioning people the creator designed. Leading Black liberation theologian,

Extraordinary Professor Anthony Reddie of the University of South Africa and the Oxford Centre for Religion and Culture expands on the definition of blackness in his presentations. His definition explains why a black theologian may enthusiastically discuss and include the Palestinian freedom struggle in their analysis of the divinely ordered black liberation pathway. He argues that Black theology expresses how black history is in fact a sacred history in God's dealings with humanity. He shows in his writings how God uses the black struggle to illustrate His design for a level of equality and reconciliation which rises above racial bigotry. Reddie's definition of blackness shows how the Palestinian struggle fits within that framework:

> *Black identities have always been diverse and complex. They defy any simplistic ways of categorizing people. The term Black has to be understood within the context of Britain and the tradition of identity politics that emerged in the 1970s. So, the term 'Black' does not simply relate to skin colour, but is rather also a political statement relating to one's sense of politicized marginalization within Britain, i.e. being 'Black' in this context is not just about those who are of 'African descent' living in the UK. It also relates to other non–White groups who suffer and experience racism (Reddie 2020).*

Certainly, the Palestinian case and the suffering they have endured under occupation, along with their proximity to Africa, places them under Reddie's definition of being politically Black. Therefore, the Palestinian cause is given a significant amount of attention in this writing as viewed from the perspective of a Black American theologian.

The nations of the world, instead of diminishing and marginalizing sets of people in order to prop up themselves, must recognize that humanity is an interconnected family, and each part of the family is important for the race's survival. This thesis will show why the familyhood of humanity is urgent and indispensable for humanity's progress and success at large. The concept of familyhood gives the idea that as human beings we are all related.

We bleed the same blood and are created by the same God. It means that the entire human race is interrelated, interconnected and interdependent. For the blessings of familyhood to be realized, there must be a willingness to look beyond self-interest and self-preservation and recognize that familyhood is in all conflicting parties' interests.

Conflict is often misunderstood. Successful conflict resolution is not achieved merely by determining who is right or wrong in a dispute but depends on courageous leadership, and the effort put forth to save, build, or restore and preserve a harmonious relationship between two conflicted parties the greater good of the community.

This thesis will highlight the need for courageous leadership for a volatile time. The fundamental causes of conflict will be analyzed. It will be seen that the same patterns and threads run through virtually all the various aspects of conflict in the world.

Conflicts that are seen today are new only as they relate to the personalities involved. The same issues that leaders face today are like those which have been witnessed in ancient times. The apostle James also refers to first-century conflicts between capital and labour that remain persistent in the postmodern world. This is found in the Bible, in the chapter in the New Testament that bears his name. The conflict among political parties today often revolves around the issues that separate capital and labour (James 5:1-9). Many militant revolutionary struggles that occur within nations grow out of the dehumanizing disregard for those with few resources and little influence. Those at the top of the economic ladder often manipulate and defraud those who are wage earners. The fact is that wage earners have so little power and influence to change their overall conditions. Revolutionary violence is often resorted to overturning the political and economic structures that have caused their suffering and dehumanization. Suppose those who have accumulated billions through the poor's labours would give attention to the Christian perspective. In that case, it could lessen the suffering and the violence that grows out of the dehumanizing factors. The epistle of James also points to this.

*Go to now, ye rich men, weep and howl for your miseries that shall come upon **you**...Behold, the hire of the labourers who have reaped down your fields, which is of you kept back by fraud, crieth: and the cries of them which have reaped are entered into the ears of the Lord of sabaoth. Ye have lived in pleasure on the Earth, and been wanton; ye have nourished your hearts, as in a day of slaughter. Ye have condemned and killed the just;* ***and he doth not resist you*** *(James 5:1-9).*

Much of the political, economic, and cultural conflicts that exist today are based on greed, an unhealthy thirst for power, and a disregard for the humanity of those considered the lesser nations, the more inferior races and the lesser classes. Those who lack resources, influence and power are deserving of equal respect and dignity, for all nations, peoples, and classes are created in the image of God. Their work, value, and contribution to the human race's furtherance should not only be appreciated but celebrated. It appears that too often, while the U.S military apparatus subjugates poorer nations, mainstream white American theologians and clergy sides with its own or are silent. This is also their common attitude when blacks in America are brutalized by a militarized police state and are targeted by a prison industrial complex. According to the Christian theological view, the Creator of the universe will judge the powerful ones who abuse and oppress those they think to be weaker. There is a higher authority to whom all-powerful nations and institutions must answer. The conflict between the economically privileged and those who are exploited due to race and class is an unequal fight. Both sides do not hold an equally moral ground. It appears that God is on the side of the weaker oppressed ones in this Conflict, and it is vital for those in power to recognize this.

1.2 Statement of the Problem

The problem that this thesis identifies is not a new one and is best explained and articulated by historical figures like Dr Martin Luther King. The idea of great nations crumbling due to separatism along with the dangers of a nuclear holocaust are given attention in this thesis and are buttressed by *"Where Do We Go from Here"* by Dr King. In that work, King emphasized the need for a "kind of positive revolution" of peace and familyhood over war. He shows how the pursuit of nuclear ambitions is a "tragic death wish (King 1967: 185)," and calls for world leaders to rearrange their priorities for the good of humanity. This unwitting death wish largely coincides with the problem that this thesis identifies and the case to be made.

Reverend King identified the hindrances to familyhood and human dignity. He often simplifies human conflict as a struggle between love and hate. He illustrates for his readers the dangers of spiritually bowing to hatred and retaliation. King holds up for his readers the examples of great nations that crumbled from within because hate was the high price, they were willing to pay. This same price of hate, according to King, is self-defeating to all who produce it. This hefty price of hate has also been paid by individuals and famous figures in history to the regret of many. This concept captures the emphasis of this thesis.

> *We can no longer afford to worship the God of hate or bow before the altar of retaliation. The oceans of history are made turbulent by the ever-rising tides of hate. History is cluttered with the wreckage of nations and individuals who pursued this self-defeating path of hate (ibid., 187).*

The progress of humanity is insecure and forever under threat because of the problem of dangerous weapons combined with heightened animosity between nations around the world. The failure to recognize the familyhood of human beings regardless of nationality places humanity in a perilous position. There is an amazing irony when one considers one of the contributing factors of dehumanization, which is racial exploitation. Much of the hate, fear and dehumanization that exists, has historically been created by a large segment of the Christian religion itself.

1.2.1 The Dehumanizing Effects of Racism and Classism and Tribalism

The problem of dehumanizing others due to racial differences or economic classism is harmful within nations. It is damaging to a nation's ability to grow and flourish, and perhaps even survive. We will not learn from one another's background, cultural perspectives and contributions. Those are most negatively impacted by racism through psychological trauma often fall short of fulfilling their potential contributions to the larger society. Those who are marginalized due to race or class are not able to make those contributions to their society that will benefit the whole. They are viewed as intellectually and culturally inferior. Racism and classism may cause a society to overlook the potential and expertise of individuals within the oppressed race.

> *All men are interdependent. Every nation is an heir of a vast treasury of ideas and labour to which both the living and the dead of all nations have contributed (King, 1967: 178).*

Such potential and expertise undiscovered may possibly be needed at any critical moment for the survival of the entire nation. The failure to recognize human interdependence is detrimental to the human family.

1.2.2 The Problem of European Theological Views of the Kingdom of God

European Christian crusades, colonialism, and the slave trade in the Americas all have connections to faulty theological perspectives. Historical European theology suggests that they (White Anglo-Saxon Protestants) are the church and the kingdom of God on Earth which must literally conquer by any means. This idea the darker-skinned nations are barbaric, savage, barely human and in need of being civilized by White Christians is racist and culturally ignorant. True Christian theology is desperately needed. Christianity at its roots began among the darker races, and desperately needs to be reclaimed by those who understand love and the familyhood of humanity. Those Christian communities who understand the pain of oppression and dehumanization may play a vital role in the fight, and their voices must come to the forefront. Too often the faces that represent Christianity to the world are European ones, and consequently the world community is reminded of the negative social impact of Eurocentric theological views. Such perspectives have historically denied human dignity to non-Europeans. Despite this, European Christianity views itself as historically doing much good for civilization. This idea must be refuted.

The late Father Michael Prior, a Roman Catholic theologian, very similarly agrees with a few previously mentioned in this thesis. He goes into detail concerning the role of Eurocentric theology as an agent of oppression. In his own way, Father Prior does not argue that the Old Testament is misunderstood but rather is mistaken in its portrayal of divinely approved wars, such as Israelite conquest of the Canaanites and the Amorites. He argues that those Old Testament stories of holy conquest should not be referenced when explaining God's character and morality. Prior's research has led him to conclude that many of the Old Testament's conquest stories were added later. He challenges theologians to examine the ministry of Jesus closely. He suggests that a simple analysis of Jesus's teachings will show that divinity would never sanction the Old Testament conquest accounts. Prior suggests that the gospel of Jesus Christ should be the focus and that international laws on human rights are more consistent with Jesus' teachings than conquest narratives and Old Testament standards. He suggests that the Old Testament conquest narratives allow for conquering inhabited lands and genocide by those who view their civilization as morally superior. He shows that this is what inspired both the crusades and the colonizing of Africa and the Americas. As the previous sources noted, Father Prior lays the blame of Palestinian suffering upon the shoulders of Christian theologians who embrace Zionism from an eschatological perspective. He shows how the Medieval Church in Rome believed they had the keys or authority of heaven to conquer through violent means. They understood theologically that they were chosen in Medieval times as the Israelites were in the Old Testament times. The Church, therefore, enlisted literal armies on their behalf. He argues that Jesus Christ should be the model rather than the Old Testament narratives of conquest and land capturing.

Prior references the papal crusaders' language who called for the liberation of Jerusalem from "unclean" races with "unclean" practices which they claimed were filing the holy land with evil and uncleanness. He showed how they used the Old Testament and justified aggression. He illustrated how they *held the testaments in one hand and a sword in the other. The conquered with the cross on the breast* (Prior 1997: 21).

Like the Old Testament conquest narratives, the Roman Church utilized religion and political power. The two were always blurred within their ecclesiastical structure. Prior shows how the concept of Rome's chosen status set the cultural foundation for the mistaken Eurocentric superiority complex. This was borrowed from Old Testament conquest theology, according to Prior. This superiority mindset bled into European society's fabric, which led them to believe that all others were unclean, savage and inferior. The savage nature of non-Europeans, (as the Church taught) made those nations worthy of being civilized through colonization, oppression, and slavery. One statement in Prior's book illustrates the theology of oppression and its origins. In each of the Old Testament conquest narratives, Prior argues, there is no sensitivity to the pain of those who have been conquered. Moreover, the stories suggest that the conquered deserve the pain they suffer. That this is the mindset of Eurocentric Christian theology, is what Prior expostulates.

The absence of concern for 'the natives' reflects the deeply ingrained Eurocentric, colonialist prejudice which characterizes virtually all historiography, as well as the discipline of biblical studies (Prior 1997: 25).

Prior calls for a theology that critiques colonialism and Zionism by the example of Jesus, which is consistent with Jesus' preferential treatment of the downtrodden by imperial powers. It is incumbent upon theologians, Christian authors and clergy to recognize their own hidden superiority complex and begin to view the scripture and theology through the eyes of the exploited and tyrannized. This was the lens through which afflicted and oppressed Christ viewed the world.

1.2.3 The Problem of Eurocentric Israelology and Eschatology

It is also essential to recognize the harmful effects of many Christian theologians burdened with an Old Testament literalist approach to the "chosen people" and "holy land" concepts. Such concepts have been the source of so much of this world's people's pain and suffering. These problems will be addressed in this thesis. R. Kendall Soulen and Linda Woodhead have compiled a substantive volume entitled "God and Human Dignity." This work helps express some of this thesis's vital issues. Until these problems within European Christian theology is addressed, it will fail to a large degree to be an agent of familyhood and reconciliation that Jesus of Nazareth commissioned His followers to fulfill (*Soulen and Woodhead, 2006: xvi.*).

"God and Human Dignity" reinforces the hypothesis which identifies the problem of European Christian theology, particularly in supporting Conflict and war which leads to landlessness. This work highlights the connection between dehumanization and landlessness. It analyzes the problem this poses for colonial Christian theology and the hope for restoration, reconciliation and familyhood. The writers of "God and Human Dignity" focuses the reader upon the refugee crisis, along with the landlessness of the Palestinian peoples. These problems largely exist because of Christian eschatology, which is primarily supported by the most powerful nation on Earth, the United States of America. This version of eschatology presents many problems. If the Hebrew Bible's God is the God who values all humanity and is the author of all humanity, he would desire that no population should wander in landlessness. These are the problems posed in *"God and Human Dignity."* This work became a valuable source for this thesis, due to the substantive arguments presented on this issue. The authors go as far as to state that the idea of possessing one's land is the central theme of biblical faith, not just for Israel, but for all people. In highlighting these issues, they tell an incredible story about the refugee crisis's extent and the dislocation dilemma. Respect and human dignity in a world that God claims as his own has much to do with having freedom and peace in one's land. The problem is dramatized in "God and Human Dignity" which points out the fact

that today's refugee and dislocation crisis has never in recorded history been at the levels which exist today.

> *The crisis challenges Christians everywhere to reflect theologically and practically about how our understanding of humanity as the image of God, might apply to masses of displaced persons existing in degraded and seemingly hopeless conditions (ibid., 135).*

It is not argued in this thesis that the Israeli needs should not be considered or addressed. The issue revolves around a faulty eschatology and a racial superiority (chosen people) tradition. These views are heavily emphasized within Western Christian theological circles, which pressure their politicians to lean unjustly in favour of the Israeli government. *God and Human Dignity* strike at the heart of this theological problem.

> *Problematic hyper-literal readings of the Bible by Christian Zionists, in which the only significant land is that of biblical (and contemporary) Israel since Jewish return and possession of this land has a cosmic, apocalyptic significance as a prelude to the second coming of Christ (ibid., 138).*

Following World War II's horrors and the inhumane genocidal treatment of the Jewish people of Europe, many Western leaders heard Zionists' cry to return Jewish refugees to the Middle East. While this effort to solve this problem had good intentions, it disregarded the Palestinian families who had historical roots in that land surrounding Jerusalem.

Would such action have ever occurred on the continent of Europe, where an entire nation would be carved out of Great Brittan? Would any European nation agree to displace a population within Europe to benefit an Asian, African or Arab population? Why didn't the Europeans carve out a slice of land within Europe for the Jewish people to relocate? Is Palestinian humanity not as valuable? These are questions that must be asked of Christian theologians. This effort to relocate the Jewish refugees to Palestine has been the source of much pain and suffering to the Palestinian people. This problem has created a ripple effect throughout the Arab and Persian world and has been the centerpiece of foreign relations for Western nations since that time. *God and Human Dignity* address this problem.

> *It simultaneously created another displacement crisis of unprecedented dimensions...the largest single group of refugees in the world today consists of millions of Palestinians Compounding the ethnic and national aspects of the Conflict are interfaith dimensions involving competing Jewish, Christian, and Muslim claims (ibid., 136).*

God and Human Dignity becomes an indispensable source material for this thesis, as it shows how Christian theology can be applied both detrimentally and beneficially for humanity. As it relates to the geopolitical arena, euro-centric theology has been most detrimental to large populations that Christ desires to save and rescue from both spiritual and physical captivity.

The pain and suffering in the Middle East, Eurocentric theology's connection to the dehumanization of the Palestinian and Arab world are analyzed in this thesis. This legacy is a barrier to the familyhood of humanity.

Father Prior makes the case that is quite useful to the main points of this thesis. He suggests (1997, p. 35) that in most cases, virtually all theologians would show compassion toward refugees and those suffering under occupation, except for the Palestinian cause. He asserts that this is because of the religious and theological demands of the Christian community. Suddenly the same people who sympathized with other population groups driven from their lands, lose their sense of compassion when it comes to the Palestinian dilemma. Any interested party would find a significant proportion of theological literature surrounding showing why Jewish people belong in Palestine. Close to zero white Christian theological literature exists that highlights the suffering of Palestinians, not even that of Palestinian Christians, who should be considered brothers and sisters in Christ. This thesis shows the need for a total self-examination by Christian theologians, an acknowledgement of error, and reconciliation efforts to achieve that familyhood. Liberation theologians must take the lead in shaping new world order.

1.2.4 Dehumanizing Theology and the Legacy of the Transatlantic Slave Trade

The same dehumanizing theology that causes so much suffering in the Middle East can be said of Africa's European treatment. This too is a barrier to familyhood. Too often, Christian theologians do not seek to understand the pain that European Christians have caused others but would rather forget and move forward.

The book, *African Humanity*, written by Dr Robinson Milwood, addresses these problems and concerns. He was a Methodist minister, who studied the Church's history in the slave trade. Dr Milwood's findings are consistent with the findings of this thesis. In 2010, this author visited Elmina Castle in Ghana, West Africa. It was a Portuguese slaveholding area. It was amazing to find that the castle was administered under the supervision and sanction of the Dutch Reformed Church. According to the tour guides, the Dutch Reform ministers would even baptize the enslaved ones in a particular section of the castle before boarding the slave ships. This same castle was used to torture and starve captured Africans who struggled for freedom in any way. This is in stark contrast to the New Testament's Jesus, who promised to set the captives free. Dr Milwood identifies the same problem areas as other scholars on this topic, including this research. In his book, *African Humanity*, he shows the Church's active involvement in the slave trade, and the extreme brutalization and dehumanization.

According to Milwood, Western Christianity was not based on the gospel of love, deliverance, and redemption but a European cultural dynamic that suggests that Christ has ordained them to conquer other races to advance the kingdom of God. This religion is not based upon the humility, self-sacrifice and service of Christ but instead based on the denial of freedom, justice and equality. Milwood suggests that slaveholder theology not only gave credence to the slave trade, but its adherents participated as a part of its world mission. It is astounding how invested Christian theology was in the indescribable horror of the transatlantic slave trade. Africans would live under the dehumanizing rod of cruelty, and the world has never been the same. Milwood identifies his own Methodist Church's role in perpetuating the myth that the trans-Atlantic slave trade was a part of God's great plan for his kingdom.

Milwood expostulates that the Methodist Church's Eurocentric theology had indeed proclaimed salvation, but a salvation which offered a cultural transformation doctrine. According to Milwood, this salvation was salvation from dignity, culture, language and spirituality. He alleges that such thoughts were the foundation of many Methodist theologians. They offered a religion of submission to the European, which required cultural assimilation and dehumanization on the African part. Additionally, Milwood details the theological-anthropological views of Europeans concerning the African race, which the Methodist church used to justify the dehumanizing practices of slavery.

> *Even the Methodist church had claimed that Africans were biologically inferior to whites. Other scholars such as the European and British scientists claimed that in the evolutionary process, Africans emerged biologically inferior* (Milwood, 2012: 55).

It has been quite a problem that the white supremacist organizations of the United States, such as the Klu Klux Klan, profess to believe in Jesus Christ. It is puzzling that one can believe in the Christ who identifies with the oppressed, and yet supports and participates in oppression. Milwood is a helpful resource in underscoring this additional barrier to reconciliation and familyhood. We find that not only was religion used to oppress, but the scientific community linked arms with the Church in giving sanction to the dehumanization of humans. The impact of this dehumanization still plays a role in the world today. It has largely been unaddressed.

1.2.5 The Dehumanizing Nature of a "Thing-Oriented" Society

The barriers to familyhood and human progress are not only seen in the history of the Transatlantic slave trade and Zionist theology, but an additional barrier exists as it relates to how the powerful manipulate the poor. A theology that suggests that material possessions and military conquests are signs of Divine favor is highly problematic. This concept is challenged by the teachings of Dr Martin Luther King. King pointed out the problems of a materialistic "thing-oriented society" versus a "people-oriented society."

Greed, power, and selfishness have been the source of much of the oppression and suffering which has existed to this day. Wars and uprisings among nations result. There are enough resources in the world to improve the lives of all its occupants. The self-regarding attitude of the powerful hurts the poor and limits the good that the powerful could accomplish. The problem is amplified by views that the structures of plantation economics and exploitative capitalism are the answers to the world's poverty problems. The fact that American and European Christianity self identifies with and helps to create such systems is the greatest of ironies. The theology that suggests that their material "blessings" are secure due to their unwavering support of hardline Israeli occupation of Palestine is inconsistent with the teachings of Jesus or any notions of human decency. Such a "thing oriented" theology has given license to unnumbered crimes against humanity.

1.3 Problem Formulation

To a significantly large degree, the survival of great nations hinges on their ability or inability to peacefully resolve conflict. Leaders in faith communities from previous generations have put their finger on the pulse of humanity's conflicts and the urgent need for solutions. Yet, their advice has often gone unheeded by contemporary leadership. These problems are more critical today, and leaders can no longer afford to ignore this field's problems. This was dramatically illustrated in a sermon (February 4, 1968) by the late American civil rights icon--Dr. Martin Luther King. It was called "The Drum Major Instinct." Once again, King illustrates the urgency of brotherhood and the acknowledgement of human interdependence.

> *I'm sorely afraid that we won't be here to talk about Jesus Christ and about God and about [familyhood] too many more years. If somebody doesn't bring an end to this suicidal thrust that we see in the world today, none of us are going to be around, because somebody's going to make the mistake through our senseless blunderings of dropping a nuclear bomb somewhere (King, 1968, "The Drum Major Instinct," Sermon at Ebenezer Baptist Church, Atlanta).*

King goes on in his speech and addresses the consequences of political/cultural domination and global war. According to King, such a conflict would stem from humanity's innate instinct to dominate and rule the world. This instinct, King suggests, may ultimately destroy civilization as it is known. King argues that the pursuit of domination combined with the failure to seek familyhood may have apocalyptic implications. King puts forward the idea that the Almighty may very well withdraw his favour from nations who dehumanize others in their pursuit of greatness. He argues that America and other nations which seek world dominance at any cost, will crumble as did Imperial Rome. The civil rights leader identified humanity's selfish pride as the culprit of the waged wars in the world. The way King saw it, was that the advancement in nuclear power, combined with the madness of world domination, and the emotion surrounding it, that a nuclear disaster could happen at any moment. For that reason, Martin Luther King cried aloud for familyhood among the races and the nations. He was afraid that in their fierce campaign for domination, combined with the normalizing of bombing other countries, the civilized world was not only dehumanizing others but was also being dehumanized. Such a scenario, King believed, could be avoided altogether through the embrace of familyhood and togetherness. King also famously compared segregation and discrimination with the spirit of militarism and violence. He stared prophetically into what he called the "abyss of annihilation" through the telescope of violence, oppression, selfishness and discrimination. In an October 15, 1962, speech, delivered by Dr King at Cornell College, Mt. Vernon, Ohio, he stated the following:

> *I am convinced that men hate each other because they fear each other. They fear each other because they don't know each other, and they don't know each other because they don't communicate with each other, and they don't communicate with each other because they are separated from each other (King, 1962). "An Address by the Reverend Dr. Martin Luther King, Jr.," Cornell College, Mount Vernon, Iowa) Dr. Martin Luther King's visit to Cornell College - Cornell College*

In this speech, King's words underline this thesis's significant points and the problems it outlines. Besides, there are even more simplistic lessons that one may learn from the discussion of Conflict and human dignity. It is helpful even at a personal level. This same hatred, prejudice, fear, and inability to peaceably settle differences has led to fractured homes, churches, religions, marriages, and communities, thus hindering progress and poses future dangers for civilization as we know it. This research will analyze the solutions to this severe and foreboding problem.

1.4 Purpose and Significance of the Study

This thesis will explore not only the symptoms of conflict, alienation, marginalization of the poor and vulnerable societies in the world as well as the root causes. Additionally, it explores the theology of reconciliation of humankind as it relates to economic systems, societal structures and international policies. In the spirit of Christian anthropology and Christological reconciliation, this thesis will identify barriers to reconciled familyhood, the urgency of confronting them and how to dismantle them with moral authority.

This thesis is designed to equip today's theologians, clergy, politicians and community leaders with a resource on how to address and confront the injustices that exist from the legacy of colonialism and slavery. Christian leaders view the injustices of the world through a theological lens, and this thesis provides the language and moral vocabulary by which to argue and work against injustice and inhumanity. Arguments are given that help to articulate the balance between forgiveness and demands for justice.

Christian leaders who desire to engage in the work of justice, and the work of Christ through reconciliation and love, will be given the language to voice both concerns. Reconciliation is the object for Christian theologians, yet injustice and dehumanization stand in the way of achieving Christological objectives. This study provides theologians and clergy a systematic way to argue in favor of reconciliation and against the evils that divide the human race. It is the Christian responsibility of theologians, clergy and religious leaders to empathize and demonstrate the compassion of Jesus by giving voice to the voiceless who suffer from dehumanization and unaddressed generational trauma. Theologians, clergy and religious leaders cannot underestimate the power of language. This thesis may assist theologians and clergy in their work for change and reconciliation through their voices. This study is significant because it provides a most valuable tool to address the urgent need for familyhood and reconciliation which additionally provides the foundation for direct action.

1.5 The rationale for the study

This thesis aims to awaken the consciousness of the political, academic, ecclesiastical and corporate elite concerning the need to address the barriers to familyhood due to the historical pain that has been brought upon the world in the last thousand years. This thesis hopes that this awakening will help those in power address global conflict from a new historical and theological perspective. Prayerfully this new perspective helps leaders approach the conflicts on the planet with a more profound sense of humility concerning the historical wrongs that have been committed without justification and defensiveness. This thesis is written to help those among the powerful nations, to see people who are not like them as one of them and not as the other. The encouragement is to walk in the shoes of others metaphorically. This thesis aims to bring about an awareness of the damaging effects of dehumanization and to see the real value from a theological perspective, of human beings of other cultures, races, tribes and languages. However, the end goal is not merely awareness, but a call to action within one's career or life mission, to address these concerns within one's capacity. This thesis's secondary goal is to see the value of human relationships and interdependence and consequently work toward resolving conflict personally. Hopefully, having read this thesis, there will be those who will benefit personally and work toward strengthening relationships and building bridges. Whether one is a prime minister, pastor or a parent, they may gain much practical knowledge concerning human relationships from this thesis.

Christian theologians would benefit from this thesis, as it will raise awareness of the damage that has been done by Eurocentric theology. Such theologians may respond by looking at the gospel of Jesus with a new outlook and perspective. Those who perhaps see how Western-based theology has contributed to pain and conflict and are interested in pursuing a non-Eurocentric theology will benefit. They will find ways to articulate their views.

Diplomats, mediators, and conflict managers will find much to utilize in this thesis to help shape their thinking related to the causes of Conflict and the fears involved. Human rights leaders and those interested in that field will find this thesis an extremely helpful resource for their career. They will see not only the symptoms of oppression but also the historical causes. Local civil rights leaders may not change the world but may indeed impact their communities. This thesis will equip them for their noble yet challenging work.

What is unique about this thesis and how it fits within theology and human dignity is significant. One will see from the sources that have been utilized in this thesis, that there has been much written about human dignity, theological anthropology, and familyhood. Often, these topics are given attention separately, but this thesis brings the three together. This research is significant in its contribution because it combines the need for conflict resolution between nations, races and classes, and on a personal practical level. It is an appeal to familyhood at all levels and gives practical wisdom based on research and expertise.

Restorative justice as it relates to reparations for the damages in the aftermath of the Trans-Atlantic Slave Holocaust, colonialism, and Palestinian displacement is given voice in this thesis as a means achieving the beloved community. Finally, this thesis also answers a challenge presented by the Catholic theologian, Father Michael Prior. Prior addresses the imbalance of theological literature surrounding showing why the Jewish people belong in Palestine, and close to zero theological literature exists that highlights the suffering of Palestinians for the purpose of Zionist ambitions (Prior, 1997: 35.) This thesis helps to fill that void.

1.6 Literature Review

Familyhood, human dignity, interdependence and conflict resolution are subjects that are interconnected. It may be argued that such concepts are mere fantasy, yet there have been glimpses of hope that such goals are achievable. Although it may be thought to be naïve or overly ambitious, familyhood and reconciliation are urgently needed. There has been much research conducted in the areas that have been mentioned. This thesis has enlisted several qualified scholars to help make this case. Several genres of literature have been explored: (1) Studies in theological anthropology (2) restorative justice (3) theological reconciliation (4) the problems of Zionism (5) human dignity.

The Cultural and Structural Barriers to Reconciled Familyhood

The literature explored does not merely identify political and cultural barriers to familyhood and reconciliation, but also the spiritual dynamics surrounding the problems of fear, hatred, love, and greed. The sources that have been utilized in this thesis are incapable of providing solutions to those spiritual problems but can raise awareness of them so that growth can happen. When analyzing the problems of race relations, colonialism, nationalism, militarism, economic oppression and war, it is safe to conclude that they are all connected. Because they are connected, they must be faced together. These are not separate problems. There is a single thread between each of them, which is the devaluation of the other's humanity. *Where Do We Go from Here: Chaos or Community (1967)* by Reverend Dr Martin Luther King masterfully shows the connection between those human problems. Dr King goes beyond race relations problems in the United States and tackles nuclear armament and global conflict. King gives practical help on how to resolve the problems of recognizing human dignity within a national landscape. Non-violent direct action is the cure that King proposes. In this book, King acknowledges that the world's issues surrounding conflict are complex and not as easily resolvable as they are on a regional level. He offers non-violent direct action as a path but stops short of working to resolve global conflicts.

The great proportion of issues surrounding respect for human dignity and familyhood are theological. A significant portion of the obstacles to peace in the Middle East is unrelated to two cultures not being able to get along with one another, but the problem of Eurocentric theology that devalues native peoples and cultures. Suppose this barrier is removed particularly within the ecclesiastical protestant community within Israel's most powerful ally, the United States, the world will be able to move toward peace and harmonious action. The theological problem of Eurocentric views of the scriptures is the idea of chosen people and holy land. The theological conclusions of American protestants have yielded unapologetic and unwavering support for Israel's state, while ignoring the suffering's plight. These views, so much unlike the Jesus of the gospels, should be abandoned and discarded. These are the problems addressed by R. Kendall Soulen and Linda Woodhead, who have compiled a substantive volume entitled *"God and Human Dignity."* They argue that there are more refugees in the world today than at any point in human history. Their solution is to counter such Eurocentric perspectives and call upon Christian theologians to re-evaluate their concept of chosen people and the holy land and work to relieve Palestinian suffering as Jesus would.

The Contribution of Liberation Theology to Human Dignity and Theological Anthropology

Liberation theology, Palestinian theology, black theology and black liberation theology have been explored as instruments to address familyhood barriers on a global level. The world that exists today and the hostilities that emerge may be traced back to the Transatlantic slave trade. This horror of the slave trade illustrates the outcome of White European theology, which tends to dehumanize as no other. This does not suggest that all White European theologians are guilty, but too many are either complicit or silent on this topic. It may be argued that the Jesus of White European theology, is not the Jesus who made men whole, but a "white plastic Jesus (Milwood, 2012: 8)" who uses his chosen culture of whiteness to save/civilize the world. These are the arguments and conclusions of author Dr Robinson Milwood in his scholarly volume entitled *African Humanity*. Milwood details the horrors of the Transatlantic slave trade and its impact on the world today. A minister in the Methodist church, Milwood shows how actively involve the Church had been in the slave trade. He illustrates how it has impacted three continents: Africa, North America and South America. Milwood further expounds on how scientists and protestant clergy came together to prove that Africans were biologically inferior and therefore their enslavement is natural. Milwood writes about how the diabolical thinking of Eurocentric Christian anthropology; they taught that in the process of evolution, black people did not complete the process as did Whites. The levels to which Africans were dehumanized are incredibly tragic, according to Milwood's depictions. Milwood proposes liberation theology and black liberation theology as the solution to counteract the European version of Jesus.

The Rwandan Genocide as a Lesson of Dehumanization Running its Full Course

Of all the massacres that have occurred in the past 50 years, none compared to the Rwandan Genocide of 1994. The international community could intervene initially, but few had the political will to get involved. This is where the issue of brotherhood comes to the forefront. If the European powers had genuinely viewed the Rwandans as brothers, would they have intervened? There are several theories about the causes of the genocide, but much is merely assumed without firsthand knowledge of the many factors involved. Some say it happened due to old hatreds between the

Hutus and Tutsis, while others say it was indoctrination and propaganda. Scott Straus was a journalist in East Africa, leading up to the Rwanda Genocide. His book, *The Order of Genocide* shows why common assumptions concerning the genocide may very well be mistaken. Straus concludes that the genocide happened within the context of a longstanding civil war. He argues that war's psychological trauma and the associated paranoia can lead any society to do the same. Straus acknowledges that media and propaganda played a role, but not to the degree that the genocide occurred. He acknowledges that there is much that both Rwandans and non-Rwandans do not know about the sociological reasons, but he believes his conclusions should be considered. His research is based on his career as a journalist who lived in east Africa and understood Rwanda's politics.

The Dehumanizing Militaristic Theology of Conquest and Expansionism

Christian theology has often glamorized the Old Testament conquest stories, including the slaughter of Israel's enemies. Extraordinarily little is stated theologically concerning the pain and suffering of the conquered. This mindset has allowed Europeans to feel justified in conquering peoples and land in the name of God. Historically speaking, Christian theology shows little to no concern for native peoples. Father Michael Prior was a Catholic theologian, who suggested that Christians should acknowledge that the Old Testament stories are problematic for human dignity and familyhood. He makes this case in his scholarly book, *The Bible and Colonialism.* He argues that European historical theology is counter to what Jesus Christ came to do. Jesus came to set captives free, make the lame walk, the blind to see, and to feed the hungry. Prior argues that historically speaking, Europeans have instead enslaved the free, disabled souls and blinded men to freedom and starved the hungry. He shows how the oppression that Palestinians suffer at the hands of the Israeli government is ignored. He criticizes the theology that labels Israel as God's chosen people and consequently have a right to the land and therefore must conquer. He concludes that there must be an awakening to the core of the gospel of Jesus, allow Him to be the example, and acknowledge

Old Testament narratives' problems. Prior doesn't show the theological issues that may arise from his critique of the Old Testament, but his points are worthy of consideration.

An additional book written by Father Prior is entitled, *"Zionism and the State of Israel: A Moral Inquiry."* This book is a major source of information and theological expression in dealing with the Israel and Palestine conflict. This volume reveals that secular Zionism predated the subsequent mainstreaming of the ideas embraced by Christian Zionism. Prior argues that Christian Zionism was developed and supported in order to give strength to the cause of secular Zionism. Prior shows the racist aspects of secular Zionism and how Christian Zionism unwittingly embraced these views. Additionally, it will be shown through this literature how many Jewish Rabbi stood against Zionism as contrary to Jewish religion and ethics.

The Perfect Love of Christ that Reconciles and Overcomes all Fear

Imaginary and genuine fear, which Christ came to eradicate (1 John 4:18) is one of the greatest hindrances to addressing past wrongs. The reasons for these fears and how to overcome them are addressed in this thesis. Marcus Buckingham is a social scientist and leadership expert who compartmentalizes commonly held universal fears in his volume *"The One Thing You Need to Know about Managing, Great Leading and Sustained Individual Success."* There is much good that is inherent in human nature, but one of the greatest weaknesses is misplaced fear. The social science which he outlines helps get the heart of racism, xenophobia, nationalism and ethnic conflict. His ideas given in his book will play a significant part in answering many issues as it relates to reconciliation and human dignity. Buckingham's discoveries will be utilized throughout this thesis.

The key to conflict resolution that leads to reconciliation is the ability to lay aside prejudice and egocentricity. When seeking solutions to the problems between parties, if the immaturity of egocentricity can be overcome, positive breakthroughs are inevitable. The book *"Getting to Yes,"* written by Roger Fisher and

William Ury, addresses the problem of ego, imaginary fears which lead to prejudice and how these matters present hindrances to reconciled communities. The co-authors are experts on negotiating tactics and the science of human relations. Their works have been used as a guide for negotiation and resolving conflicts around the world.

The Voice of Palestinian Christian Theologians Should Be Respected.

It is quite ironic that white Evangelical Christian theologians' voices are most prominent as it relates to the Middle East Conflict. Most do not reside in the Middle East where they are able to gain a firsthand account of the violence and suffering which exists in that part of the world. Many westerners are unaware that there is a historic Christian population living in Jerusalem, Bethlehem, Jericho, Nazareth and other historic places in Palestine. It may be observed that Palestinian clergy and theologians are not given the international platform of which they are worthy. This thesis seeks to give voice to their experiences, observations and theology. Their theological views are not only helpful in resolving the Palestinian and Israeli conflict but are incredibly valuable in helping overcome oppression and dehumanization wherever it exists in the world. Naim Stephan Ateek is a respected Palestinian theologian whose two volumes are utilized extensively in this thesis. One book was published in 2014 entitled *Justice and Justice Only.* While most leaders view the Palestinian and Israeli Conflict through the lens of security and conflict resolution, Dr. Ateek approaches the problems as a matter of justice. If justice is exercised, every other good will fall in place. Additionally, Ateek wrote a masterpiece entitled *"A Palestinian Theology of Liberation"* which delves into the connection between the suffering of Jesus and the suffering of Palestinians. This masterpiece will show how Palestinian oppression and persecution is more akin to the experience of Jesus of Nazareth than the militaristic theology of Western evangelicals. Liberation from occupation in the Palestinian territories is consistent with a Christ who came to set captives free and elevate the divine dignity of suffering humanity.

Mitri Raheb is another Palestinian theologian who is highlighted in this thesis. Two of his volumes are given voice. His book, *Faith in the Face of an Empire* draws striking parallels between the Roman occupation during the time of Christ's earthly ministry and the Western backed Israeli occupation of Palestine today. He shows how theology is abused to provide cover for injustice and justify expansionism. He also challenges the lack of sympathy and compassion on the part of Western theologians concerning the Palestinian plight and their misdirected focus on western ideals and misguided eschatological concepts. He seeks to make visible what seems to be invisible to Eurocentric theologians, which is the suffering of Jesus in the person of Palestinian humanity. Similarly, *Faith in the Face of an Empire,* Raheb has also written *"The Cross in Contexts: Suffering and Redemption in Palestine.* Raheb shows the connection between Jesus' suffering, shame and dehumanization on the cross and the suffering of Palestinians. He tells the story of how the cross and God's identification with human suffering at the hands of unjust principalities, appeals even to non-Christians. To dismiss the pain of Palestinian suffering is to dismiss the pain of Jesus upon the cross is the point that Raheb eloquently makes. His views which are expressed in this volume are utilized throughout this thesis.

The theology of Palestinian Bishop Munib Younan is also given attention in this thesis. Younan is bishop emeritus of the Evangelical Lutheran Church in Palestine and is a respected voice on the topic human rights and liberation for Palestinians. One notable article Younan wrote in 2017 condemned Eurocentric theology which calls for unconditional support of Israel and fails to demonstrate justice and compassion for the Palestinian community. The article was written in the Journal of Lutheran Ethics, entitled *"An Ethical Critique of Christian Zionism."* Younan argued that Christian Zionism is spiritually and ethically bankrupt and represents a false version of what Christianity is all about. He states that Christian Zionism misrepresents the work of Jesus. The spirit of his theology can be summed up in his following words: *"The story of Jesus shows us an ethic of transformation; from death to life, from sickness to healing, from oppression to freedom, from guilt to forgiveness, from inequality to justice and from hatred to peace."* Younan's "Critique" is given prominence in this thesis as it addresses the universal issues of dignity, human freedom and familyhood.

Restorative Justice and Repair

There have been many books written about reparations and restorative justice, but few have made the theological contribution to this topic as Duke L. Kwon and Gregory Thompson. Kwon and Thompson have given tremendous insight into this topic with the book cowritten by them entitled *"Reparations: A Christian Call for Reparations and Repair."* An entire chapter in this book will address the topic of reparations from a theological perspective, and the authors' ideas will be referenced in this thesis. Kwon and Thompson show that there can be no true familyhood and reconciliation without confession and repentance of past injustices and compensation given for generational theft in this post-slavery and post-colonial world. According to these authors, 18th and 19th century Chrisitan writers and abolitionists argued on behalf of reparations for enslaved persons and their descendants. These are not new ideas only recently being advanced but belong to a long history of Christian theology. Kwon and Thompson believe that there is a reason why many other groups that have suffered oppression, have been compensated, while the children of Africa throughout the world have been denied. They show that such denials are due to not fully appreciating black humanity at the same level as others.

Getting to the Promised Land is written by Rev. Dr. Kenneth Cosby who details the theft that has occurred as it specifically relates to the descendants of enslaved persons in America. Cosby shows why such a debt is owed to these descendants from a theological perspective. Cosby sets forth that the debt that is owed involves much more than the injustices of the slavery period, but also subsequent events of generational theft in America's history which are often unaddressed.

The models set forth in this thesis surrounding reparations may also apply to other places on the globe where generational robbery has occurred. It may also be applied to the Palestinian plight and all who have suffered under colonialism and have endured exploitation by the great nations of the earth.

1.7 Research Goal

The primary goal of this study is to highlight the problems of human Conflict, the negative impact of dehumanization, the ill effects of Eurocentric theology and to inspire a new generation of bold and courageous leaders who will be equipped through this research. Prayerfully this research will help theologians, Christian politicians, clergy and laypersons to identify problem areas and potential for Conflict within a community or system. It is hoped that this study will encourage a theological awakening of those under the influence of historic westernized theology. The thesis is to help leaders implement methodologies and findings to inspire peace and familyhood around the world.

1.8 The Contribution of the Study to Systematic Theology

Theological anthropology is an extremely vital branch of systematic theology. This branch of systematic theology is given substantive attention in this thesis. Several books are cited within these pages show great respect for theological anthropology. Theological anthropology is demonstrated in this thesis to be the foundation of human dignity and familyhood. What exactly is theological anthropology? It is explained and defined in the following statement:

> *In Genesis 1:26-27 the nature and worth given to human beings by divine creation is designated by the term "image of God." The notion has always been the central theme of theological anthropology. From the patristic to the modern period Christian theology has connected the dignity of human nature with the theme of the image of God (Soulen and Woodhead 2006: 9).*

This concept of theological anthropology is given its name in contrast with classical studies in the field of anthropology. Classical anthropology simply studies human beings scientifically without the benefit or burden of exploring the spiritual nature of humans and their divine origin. Theological anthropology, however, unapologetically explores the spiritual side of the topic as it relates to the image of the divine present in all humans. Christian apologist, Dr. Eric Mason, defines theological anthropology in terms of how Christians should view their own worth and that of others. According to Mason, understanding theological anthropology shapes one's view of injustices committed against fellow members of the human family:

> *Christian anthropology is grounded in the doctrine of the imago dei (Gen. 1:27). As a human being, I am created in God's image and likeness. I am his vice-regent. This role is not unique to me; I share it with all human beings. Under God, we are equal in worth and dignity. Accordingly, injustice, both from me and toward me, is objectively wrong. Such a view is true, coherent within the Christian worldview, and existentially viable for all humanity (Mason 2021: 226).*

A casual observer my conclude that the idea that all humans have equal dignity and possess the image of God is an elementary concept. One may assume that the Christian view of anthropology is embraced by all. However, this assumption is uninformed and naive. The idea of race is itself a human construct and cannot be found in the Christian Bible. The New Testament anthropology suggests that there is only one true race, which is the human race. Gospel writer Luke declares concerning human creation that God *"... hath made of one blood all nations of men, for to dwell on all the face of the earth, and hath determined the times before appointed, and the bounds of their habitation: (Acts 17:26)."* It must be understood that the creation of racial categories was a diabolical attempt to separate humans into various species of beings with some having a more superior status on the value chain than the other. Kant was one of the first to introduce the idea of racial categories in this way. His ideas, though contrary to Old and New Testament anthropology, gained acceptance among many Christians. Kant, an atheist, lectured widely on the topics of anthropology and geography. He is considered one of the fathers of scientific racism, advancing ideas and theories of sub-personhood.

Such views were utilized as justifications for oppression, slavery, conquest, and generational theft.

> *While he argued that humans represent a unified species, he recognized that they were divided into four races, with characteristic differences based on climate. Not surprisingly, Kant considered "the Negro race" the lowest in the human hierarchy. It should be noted, however, that Native Americans, though not classified as one of the four main races, were considered by Kant to be beneath "Negroes (Douglas 2021: 40)."*

Since the Creator authors all human life, all human life should be valued and respected. To do otherwise is to show irreverence to the Creator of human life. This thesis will highlight how much of white Protestant Christianity's eschatology is inconsistent with correct theological anthropology. Theologian and Methodist minister, Robinson A. Milwood, adds that this faulty theological anthropology has led to an erroneous soteriology (a branch of theological study of salvation).

> *The crime of African enslavement with the immoral fallacy that African...God appointed Europeans and British to impart civilization and salvation to Africans through brutalization, dehumanization, and enslavement with theological justification (Milwood 2012: 55).*

This thesis will theorize how Europeans used anti-gospel anthropology to give gravity to a racist eschatology. The approach to true theological anthropology will counter the lingering effects of the anthropology of colonial times. It cannot be overemphasized the depth of dehumanization through corrupt anthropology as detailed by Robinson Millwood, and how closely aligned ecclesiastical organizations were to the views of Kant.

> *Even the Methodist church had claimed that Africans were biologically inferior to whites. Other scholars such as the European and British scientists claimed that in the evolutionary process, Africans emerged biologically inferior (Ibid., 55).*

Some may argue that this type of anthropological thinking is limited to colonial times. However, it will be shown that the adverse effects of this remain and how there has been little done to correct the record and to acknowledge the theological and practical wrongs which have been committed. Robert Morris, a popular anti-racist white evangelical pastor, describes succinctly why racism and Christian anthropology are at odds. He says *racism questions God's creation* (Morris 2017: Sermon).

Another mistaken theological concept surrounding anthropology is the idea of the Creator making the Jews supreme over the surrounding nations. This has led to much of the suffering and oppression in the Middle East today. That the Jews had the divine right to occupy Palestine and dislocate millions in 1948 to establish the state of Israel is erroneous eschatology. This type of eschatology is based on faulty anthropology. All men are created equal and deserve remaining in their homes, raising their families and carrying out their occupations in freedom. To occupy, dislocate, dehumanize and demonize the Palestinian people is to show contempt and disrespect toward the author of their humanity. This thesis will explain the connection between faulty eschatology and misguided unwitting anthropology.

Eschatology is one of the main points covered by this thesis. The first eschatological emphasizes the ultimate destiny of humanity, which is reflected in the redemption narrative. Humankind was created in the image of his Creator, yet through the fall, he has fallen short of the glory of God. In the future, when the impact of the gospel story is ultimately realized, humanity will be restored to his creation experience due to redemption. The gospel transforms humanity, and spiritually moves him into God's original intent to create humankind. This concept is referenced in the book God and Human Dignity, one of the primary sources of this thesis.

> *Paul thinks of humans as image of God in their created identity. But it is an identity that in human historic life has not been actualized. It is by the transformative power of the gospel that human beings are progressively conformed and*

transformed to the self they are created to become (Rom. 8:29; 1 Cor.15:49-51; 2 Cor.3:18), a transformation that is consummated eschatologically (God and Human Dignity, 2006: 15).

This thesis will seek to correct the many eschatological misconceptions surrounding Israel's destiny in Palestine and the ecclesiastical role of the Church. This discussion may be controversial but is indeed necessary and urgent. This urgency is due to oppression that so many suffer as a result of mistaken eschatology. This will prove to be a valuable contribution within both Protestant and Christian circles as it tends to disagree with commonly held notions that need to be explored.

Additionally, this thesis contributes to the theology of Christology. It is unique in that it expands upon what is meant by the "white plastic Jesus (Milwood 2012: 5)" referred to by Milwood and contrasts this Eurocentric view of Jesus with the authentic Jesus of compassion, restoration, and liberation. The relationship of human liberation and the resurrection of Christ will be thoroughly examined. Furthermore, this thesis will show how ecclesiology, eschatology, Christology, and theological anthropology connect. A more enlightened understanding of biblical anthropology will aid in establishing the role of the Church and will help reshape ecclesiological perspectives.

> *Suppose the cross and resurrection of Christ point to the fact that God re-creates human dignity where it has been violated and abused. In that case, the Church which claims to be the Church of Christ is committed to sharing the situation of those who have lost their dignity in human eyes and to communicating to them the message that their dignity is re-created by the one who first bestowed it upon them (Soulen and Woodhead, 2006: 32).*

This thesis's theological aim is to challenge those European views of theology and move these discussions further in the direction of human dignity. This thesis contends that Eurocentric eschatology, ecclesiology, and Christology have been harmful in articulating theological anthropology. Additionally, it has been politically and culturally destructive, historically speaking, and has presented a barrier to familyhood and reconciliation on Earth. The theological perspectives in this study will be useful in both seminaries and human rights panels and forums.

1.9 Practical Value of the Study

The concepts in this thesis may be used in sermons, lectures and speeches by those who desire to make arguments from liberation theology and social justice. This study will provide a practical value that will assist leadership in varied arenas, such as educators, corporate officers, laborers, clergyman, parishioners, activists, government officials, and marriage partners. Each may utilize this comprehensive study to implement change, better understand the dynamics of Conflict, and use the best methods for conflict resolution to advance the aims of varied organizations in a peaceable environment with the least amount of tension and hostility.

1.11 Viability of Research

The theories outlined in this research have been proven effective both in ancient times and in this contemporary age. This research has practical value and utilizes sources which bring to view real world situations that support the suppositions which are offered. As a result of the proven effectiveness of the methods given in this study, the reader who desires to effect change in the arena of human dignity, reconciliation and restorative justice may feel confident that the sources are accurately cited, credible, easily accessible and can easily be investigated.

1.13.3 Research Setting

This research is conducted from the perspective of a black American clergyperson living in a society dominated by those of European ancestry with a history of slavery, racism, and oppression. Presently, the United States is engulfed in a sociological and political struggle involving voting rights, police brutality and killing of unarmed black people. Those who are involved in this struggle to end such violence against black citizens by the state often align with the movement slogan Black Lives Matter. Simultaneously, while protests are happening around the country, both blacks and whites are studying the sociological and the theological roots of these problems. Undoubtedly, these present conditions and lived experiences are important contributions to this research and relevant to the current state of the world. In this respect, the positionality of the researcher serves as motivation and perspective on this topic.

> *Positionality refers to the researcher's role and identity in relation to the context and setting of the research specifically. For example, you could be a practitioner in the setting, located as an expert, a combination of insider or outsider to the setting, a supervisor of employees, a member of community involved in the research, someone who shares a cultural or ethnic relationship with participants, and so on (Ravitch 2019: 45).*

As an American clergyperson of more than thirty years, the writer has had to deal with the effects of racial injustice and separation. Parishioners and church goers have for many years approached the researcher about how this topic has impacted their lives. The researcher has counseled, interceded in prayer, and publicly advocated for church members who have suffered name calling, police brutality and job discrimination. The writer has also suffered discriminatory practices such as being followed by the police for being in the "wrong" neighborhood or followed around by suspicious store owners while shopping. The frequent stopping and being questioned, which does not occur as often in white communities in the US, has been the researchers personal experience. While in primary school as a youngster, the researcher noticed how white students were not judged or penalized as harshly as black students. The difference in treatment was obvious as early as kindergarten, where it was noticeable that during certain classroom subjects, black children and white children went to separate rooms. Presently, the researcher observes that local school boards are now banning books about black history and are also targeting black teachers who speak on racial injustice. Quite recently Haitian refugees fleeing violence in South America were chased down and driven back by horse riders with whips, which was a stark reminder of slavery times. This is the case, while White Cubans are welcomed with open arms. The writer is a son of parents who grew up in America during the period of Jim Crow segregation, and the stories they told have also had a tremendous impact.

This thesis' research methods are academically sound and relevant to today's world. A plethora of primary sources in the field of sociology, and history and theology are thoroughly analyzed from the perspective of the researcher. Such a social location may contribute to bias. However, in order to counteract this bias, the author has consulted authors outside of the American civil rights movement and the Black Lives Matter movement. In analyzing the Palestinian freedom struggle, which is outside of the American experience, the researcher finds similar ideas and conclusions among Palestinian theologians. Therefore, such views are not limited to social biases within a certain location. It must also be pointed out that the author, while seeming to generalize, there is an awareness of white Evangelicals who are indeed antiracist and advocates for justice. The author serves at a university where a white colleague who is both a professor and pastor, who was threatened in the late 1980s by Klu Klux Klan, a white anti-black terrorist group. Sadly, these Klu Klux Klan terrorists, were members of his own church, who sought to close a day care center where black children were being served by the pastor. They also forbade any black families from joining the church. There have always been White Christians, such as Viola Liuzzo, who was murdered by the Ku Klux Klan, who participated in the American Civil Rights Movement.

When the writer of this thesis addresses the white Evangelical Church, or European Christianity, this should not be meant to understood that all members and churches are racially insensitive and antagonistic toward others. It simply means that far too many either unwittingly advocate for injustice, do not sympathize with victims of injustice, or do not stand up for justice. This has been the perception of black leaders in America for generations, including Dr. Martin Luther King in his writings and letters. Both the researcher and the community represented are aware of many brave white Christian leaders who have advocated for liberty for black people. They are not included in the general critique of Eurocentric Christianity and the White American Evangelical church but are considered separate from the mainstream. In this thesis, the writer will reference Robert Morris, a major White evangelical voice in America. He similarly critiques his fellow Evangelicals in addressing their attitudes toward black protestors. Although, he is antiracist, he generalizes the problem and groups himself with those he criticizes. He refers to White people and the church as the source of this problem within the American context.

> *I think we're ignorant of the problem and the depth of it…I'm talking about white people now. It means we're just ignorant…And that's me too. I've been learning some things for the past several years as I've met with pastors and friends of mine to help me understand and it has now become personal to me, not just an issue (Morris 2017: Sermon).*

In this thesis, it will be pointed out that there were White American church fathers who advocated for reparations for the formerly enslaved. Mention is also made of the great work of white abolitionists. So, in this American context, "the church" or "European Christianity" is indeed a general statement, but the generalization should be understood not to include all but represents a highly discouraging proportion. While the White Evangelical Church is criticized in this thesis, the researcher has personally observed the white evangelical pastor of the largest church in the United States, Joel Osteen, participate in the Black Lives Matter march in Houston Texas. Additionally, during a time of racial strife and white backlash from seminary professors under the guise of discrediting Critical Race Theory, noted white evangelical professor Joel Gregory condemned his professor colleagues (Gregory 2020).

The National Association for the Advancement of Colored People (NAACP) in the United States, the oldest civil rights organization, included both Christian Whites and Blacks in its early founding. They should be noted and celebrated, while simultaneously bringing one's own experiences and personal observations into the research. Additionally, while this is the lens through which the researcher views this particular topic, it should also be understood that race is not the only cause of conflict. It is the angle the writer has chosen to pursue.

2 THE UNDERLYING FEARS WHICH LEAD TO CONFLICT

2.1 Fear as a Foundation for All Conflict

When analyzing the sources and root causes of conflict, one must consider that there are invisible reasons that are often overlooked. It is often that the obvious reasons receive more attention than the more subtle reasons.

The root causes of disputes may very well lie in what are called "universal fears." Wars and global tensions often happen because of those fears. Sociologists have discovered that throughout history and among all cultures, tribes and language groups there are shared needs and fears that all of humanity hold in common. Those fears are as follows: fear of death, fear of the outsider, fear of the future, fear of chaos and fear of insignificance. If these universal fears are probed more deeply, one might be able to discover the fountain from which springs all conflicts among peoples and nations.

If the nations of the world would examine more closely the fear that exists among humankind, the human populace will get closer to that day of familyhood of humanity and avoid that "suicidal thrust," and the global "abyss of annihilation" that Dr. King spoke about. The pride and arrogance existing among nations and tribes, and the failure to seek familyhood can all be traced back to innate fears. The "drift" toward nuclear exchanges among nations which Dr. King addressed may also traced back to the same fears which have been the catalyst to all terrible wars that have been launched.

It is of vital interest that ministers of diplomacy should analyze this pervasive fear, as it may resolve many of the conflicts that are being fought or may potentially be fought in the world today. If one can learn about the fears of others rather than only focusing on their own fears, this may very well resolve many of the perplexities and tensions which exist. Therefore Dr. King implored his audience to "add the other-regarding dimension to the self-regarding dimension," and to "respect the dignity and worth of every human personality." Dr. King's theory says that it all begins with fear. He declares that men go from not communicating, and not communicating leads to unfamiliarity, and unfamiliarity leads to fear and fear leads to hatred. If the source of fear can be understood, then the other issues will be better understood in the context of those fears. Gallup's social science researcher, Marcus Buckingham identifies and addresses the five universal fears in his book called "The One Thing." Those five fears are identified as follows:

1) Fear of death—Preference for our own future and that of our own children—Nepotism springs from this fear

2) Fear of the Outsider—Societies make distinctions between those who are part of the group and those who aren't, and we are always biased in favor of the former

3) Fear of the Future—Every society is anxious about the future, and views it as unstable, unknown, and potentially dangerous.

4) Fear of Chaos--The world we know is defined by the opposite of the chaos, darkness, and disorder that preceded it.

5) Fear of Insignificance—The need for respect

(Buckingham 2005: 140-142).

Critics of Christian theology often refer to conflict narratives in scripture to suggest that such theology endorses conquest of native lands and war as an appropriate means to advance "the kingdom of God," as well as to resolve conflict. However, this is far from being the case. While such narratives have been used by Christian rulers to justify greed and conquest, such cannot be justified by the scriptures. Old Testament conflict narratives are more descriptive of the ancient world and their theological understanding rather than prescriptive of what ought to be. In fact, what is often ignored is the fact that ancient Israel was more closely related to surrounding tribes and communities than initially understood. Sometimes a casual observer may be mistaken by viewing outside communities as the "other;" while it may be that what is thought to be the "other" is simply an extension of ourselves. This is the misconception anciently and continues through contemporary times.

> *The differences between Israelites and other Canaanites from the vantage point of modern interpreters is small. Available archaeological evidence indicates that the Israelites arose indigenously in the Levant, practiced religion in a way typical of Levantine peoples, and that the Hebrew language itself is a "Canaanite" dialect. Israelite culture is a variation of Canaanite culture (Rainey 2018: 22).*

The narratives about Israel's battles must not be utilized to justify war and genocide against "foreign" enemies under divine direction. A closer look at the ancient narratives might lead one to discover that military conflicts never ultimately resolve disputes, advance the ultimate interests of the aggressor nor guarantee security. Old Testament history of military conquest illustrates how cycles of conflict and violence tend to perpetuate themselves and engender greater fears and insecurity for generations yet unborn. The eschatological lesson of scripture is that the real battles are mental and spiritual. The real battle is against fear, which Christ came to destroy. In fearing and seeking the destruction of the foreigner, one unknowingly commits destruction of themselves. All humanity is related and interdependent. The problem is that nation-states do not often see themselves in others. The human race is more related than understood or appreciated. Despite language barriers, cultural differences and geographical distances, humans are all more alike than different. Jesus Christ is depicted as the Prince of peace, who fought spiritual battles rather than physical ones and told his followers that we are all neighbors who should love one another. The Matthean record (Matthew 1:21) illustrates how Christ broke into history to save his people (Israel) from their sins of inhumanity, religious arrogance, injustice, exploitation, and disloyalty to the God of love. Historically speaking, these sins led the Israelites into unending cycles of apostasy, subjugation, and bondage. The way to break the cycle of human conflict and insecurity in Christ day as well as on a contemporary universal level is to embrace those heavenly values of love and humility which Jesus magnified during his earthly ministry. Salvation for the nations of the world comes through righteousness. The wise man agrees. *Righteousness exalteth a nation, but sin is a reproach to any people (Proverbs 14:34).* It is suggested in this thesis that the nations of the world will not be saved by murderous weapons of war but the weapons of love and faith in each other. The nations will not be ultimately secure through denying the dignity and humanity of others, but by the righteous reverencing of their dignity and humanity as sacred and godlike. Anything less than this form of righteousness would be the international sin of injustice and apostasy against a God of love which will lead to the one's own disgrace and ruination.

2.2 The Preservation of Self-dignity Does not Require the Denial of Dignity to Others

The fear of insignificance and chaos are natural to all humanity. At a deeper level, because of years of demonization of the other party, it is almost embarrassing to sit publicly and discuss hot button issues with such a demonized group. It is almost as if one is affirming the humanity and legitimacy of one who has so scornfully been depicted as unworthy of respect. It is the fear of looking weak that has kept many of the great nations of the world from sitting down with national leaders who have been presented to the public as dictators, totalitarian and murderous. The universal appeal of religion also shows this need for prestige and respect.

> *The religions that have swept the world, such as Christianity, Islam, Judaism, and Hinduism, are successful*

precisely because they offer a way-membership in the chosen race, and afterlife, a second go-round at this life— for even people with the least earthly prestige to get respect (ibid, 141).

The source of hardline animosity between nations grows more out of fear than hatred. It is true that hatred is real; but hatred is the fruit rather than the root of the problem. If fear can be lessened, the cause of hatred diminishes. Fear can make its object unnecessarily larger and life and more threatening to the beholder. When the fear is gone, the opposing party is no longer viewed as a threat to one's pride or their existence. The walls of fear that have taken many years to build do not fall over night. It takes time, effort, and patience. The alternative to making such an effort to understand the humanity of a perceived enemy is better than the risk of avoiding communication and contact.

The more one comes into face-to-face contact with an enemy, it helps one to see more of the human qualities of that enemy and less of the perceptions that rhetoric has created. It is easier to be disrespectful when one is oceans apart than when sitting around a table together. The more opposing parties sit together, the more they can build mutual understanding and trust between each other. It is better to spend time getting to know each other, than to begin immediately to deal with the perplexing issues that divide the parties. The fears must first be dealt with. The ego of each party must be appreciated and protected by the other, and after time for friendship and understanding has passed, the effort to protect the ego of the other becomes much easier.

They have egos that are easily threatened...People tend to assume that whatever they fear, the other side intends to do...It is all too easy to fall into the habit of putting the worst interpretation on what the other side says or does. A suspicious interpretation often follows naturally from one's existing perceptions (Ury and Fisher 1981: 19-22).

Learning the art of preserving and defending the dignity of human neighbors is paramount. When understanding the familyhood of all peoples, when we defend the dignity of our enemies, we are defending our own dignity. What is often overlooked is that we are all one gigantic human family with the same desires for dignity and significance in the world. One act of indignity against another may well have a ripple effect that will create a world where human dignity and worth is not appreciated. When others see that their dignity is respected, they are more inclined to listen and understand. When one sees the humanity of the other, they are more inclined to hear their stories and their pain. Perception is the key to a united humanity, and misperception is the catalyst of fear and a disrupter of social harmony.

One notable author, Dr. Robert P. Jones, an expert of religious studies, writes about the fear of white America concerning its perceived loss of political, economic and cultural dominance in the U.S. He is the CEO of Public Religion Research Institute (PRRI) which studies the intersection of culture, demographic changes, religion and theology. He has written extensively on this topic. One of his books *"The End of White Christian America"* which has been widely praised. In another volume, *White Too Long, which* he has authored he writes eloquently about how white Christian America views black equality as a threat to its dominance and are fearful of losing it. He expounds on the history of white Christian America, and how it has viewed itself as the guardian of white culture and its right to rule over black people. He explains how the preservation of its supremacy is the heartbeat of white Christian theology. Black people are a small minority but have accomplished amazing feats and have climbed the ladders of political power despite the obstacles of discrimination. Even though, black people in America are a small minority, White's fear of losing its grip on power are extremely real. According to Jones, White ecclesiology and its theological circles are the driving forces in its quest to resist calls for greater equality. Jones further adds:

American Christianity's theological core has been thoroughly structured by an interest in protecting white supremacy. The unsettling truth is that, for nearly all of American history, the Jesus conjured by mostly white congregations was not merely indifferent to the status quo of racial inequality; he demanded its defense and preservation as part of the natural, divinely ordained order of things (Jones 2020: 17-18).

Fear of chaos and insignificance (loss of cultural dominance) often leads to authorities and authoritarianism is maintained by fear. Those who fear cultural diversity from outsiders and have the tendency to view such demographics as chaotic are numerous. Those who share such fears are often attracted to political strong men who promise to stand up for them against the changing world and demands of others for equality. It is this fear, by white Christian America, according to Jones that led to the election of Donald Trump as the president of the United States in 2016. His open support of police brutality, his dehumanizing commentary on African nations, his verbal assault on black athletes for their activism, his dehumanizing commentary on Mexican immigrants, and his promise to ban immigrants and travelers from Muslim countries in the name of national security was quite appealing to white Christians in America. Many political candidates had promised to end abortions in the America's modern history, but Trump channeled a new energy that heretofore had not been seen. His promise to stand up against these forces and to restore America back to a more well-ordered society before Muslims and Mexicans began to immigrate and before African Americans began to protest police brutality. Trump's campaign would remind many of the times when the cultural and racial hierarchy lines were more defined and were fearful of losing. Jones gives many clues about what separated Donald Trump from other candidates in the minds of white American Christian voters.

> *Through appeals to white supremacy... which was primed for receptivity by the perceived external threat of racial and cultural change in the country... he evoked powerful fears about the loss of white Christian dominance amid a rapidly changing environment (Jones 2020: 27).*

Those in the predominantly white Christian culture in the United States may argue that their fears are not about preserving their past dominance, but of losing a culture of moral goodness for one that is evil. Amazingly, white Christian culture conveniently ignores the evils of both its past and present. From their perspective, calls for social justice and civil rights have a direct connection to sexual promiscuity, abortion, drug addiction, gang violence and juvenile delinquency. They also fear that an undue emphasis of civil rights and compassionate immigration laws will cause millions of Muslims to immigrate to the United States, thus making it a non-Christian, and Muslim friendly country. The idea is that the call for equality and social justice is the gateway to undermining a Christian society and creating a godless one. While fearing a Christless culture, White evangelical Americans seem unaware of the Un Christlike character of their positions, and the cry of Jesus who said, "When I was a stranger, you did not welcome me." Moreover, White Christian America, to a large extent has resisted any criticism of its Christless actions in its own history, which are far greater evils than the imagined ones it fears. Many would rather forget about the genocide of native American populations, the transatlantic slave trade, family separation for hundreds of years, animalistic breeding of its slave population, lynching, burning down of prosperous black villages, deadly medical experimentation, segregation and police violence. According to Jesus, it is difficult to see the "mote" in one's neighbors' eye, when one has an obstruction in ones' own eye, and one should remove his own visual obstruction, before he can criticize another (Luke 6:41.) The great liberation theologian, James Cone addresses the reasons why American churchpersons resist calls for black empowerment.

> *That most churches see an irreconcilable conflict between Christianity and Black Power is evidenced not only by the de facto segregated structure of their community, but by their typical response to riots: "I deplore the violence but sympathize with the reasons for the violence." Churchmen, laymen and ministers alike apparently fail to recognize their contribution to the ghetto condition through permissive silence— (Cone 2018: 36-37).*

To criticize and deplore how people react to their pain and oppression and fail to consistently criticize the abuses that lead to such expressions of discontent is hypocritical. We are all one human family. There is no need to fear the empowerment of others. When the weak are empowered, all humanity benefits from their contribution to the whole. It is a sign of strength and progress when a community can acknowledge their contribution to societal pain and labor for the empowerment of those that have been weakened. Working on behalf of the powerless does not disempower the dominant society but empowers our common humanity. Embracing the dignity of another never threatens the dignity of oneself, but an acknowledgment of one's own dignity. This is important to understand from a Christological standpoint. Rather than viewing one another as potential threats, we ought to welcome one another, as Christ reached out to the alienated human race who were once enemies and welcomed them into his kingdom.

> *He practiced unconstrained hospitality, inviting to his table people whom nobody thought could be saved, people whom nobody wanted saved...Jesus was other than the God we expected. This is the Christological basis for Paul's command to the church in Rome: "So welcome each other, in the same way that Christ also welcomed you, for God's glory" (Rom 15:7 CEB) (Willimon 2016: 16-17).*

If it were true that one's own dignity is dependent on the dehumanization and disrespect of the other, this would be an insult to one's own dignity. Duke University's professor of Christian Ministry, Dr. William Willimon addresses the Christological error of self-justification and attitudes of moral superiority in relationship to others in his scholarly volume, *No Fear in Love*. He writes about how white Christian politicians boast about how America should never apologize for its present or past actions, due to this mindset of moral exceptionalism. Such attitudes contradict the Christological truths they claim to believe in and represent. Confession, sorrow for sins committed and harms inflicted upon others is a thread that runs throughout scripture.

More than one presidential candidate has recently bragged, "I will never apologize for America." Christians, based on the great grace we have received from Christ, are always apologizing, confessing, and repenting... I am the enemy of God. I am the one who by my lifestyle and choices make myself a stranger to my sisters and brothers. I'm free to admit that because, in spite of my hostility to God, Jesus Christ has received me as friend. I am also the one who has received grace and revelation from the Other (Willimon 2016: 14).

The attitude that says we have done too much good to apologize and correct historical wrongs is a sign of arrogance and not the humility that Jesus of Nazareth envisioned for his followers. This lack of self-criticism oftentimes causes one to see flaws and evils in others even when the perceived flaws and evils do not exist. After the terrorist attacks on the United States, noted liberation theologian, Jeremiah Wright called for America to examine its actions internationally as one of the primary root causes of terrorism around the world. The attitude of White Christian America is that it is a force for good in the world, should never be blamed for political violence, and that there is no moral equivalence of America's evils and the evils of other nations. Dr. Wright disagreed with this idea, and it is often the case that politically engaged black Americans also disagrees. Dr. Wright happened to be the pastor of soon to be senator and eventual president of the U.S., Barack Obama. During the election campaign of then American senator, Barack Obama, the American political right wing, dominated by white Christians, discovered the sermon of Obama's pastor. In that sermon, Wright declared, "God Damn America." The video clip of Wright declaring these words were repeatedly played on American televisions. This sermon was used as a political weapon against then Senator Obama, by both the presidential campaign of Hillary Clinton and the American Christian right. The idea that Obama's political enemies desired to communicate by referencing the sermon, is that Obama did not love America and wanted it to be damned. It was quite ironic that in 2007, an African American candidate was being disqualified for being a member of a church that dared remind America of its evil past. Obama's political enemies designed to portray him as a rebellious black person who was unthankful to live in what they perceived as a good and prosperous country. The Christian right were amazed that one could say *"God Damn America"* when God is on the side of Christian America. Wright's sermon was used to cause white Christian America to be fearful of Barack Obama. What is also quite shameful about how the political class used the sermon of Reverend Wright, is their immediate reaction to generate fear in the eyes of the public, rather than examining the entire context of the speech, and the Christian theology behind it. Further analysis of the sermon would have revealed that Wright was basing the premise of his argument by agreeing with words of a distinguished American diplomat, Edward Peck. The statement that Peck made concerning America reaping the whirlwind of its own actions on September 11, 2001, were made on a popular Christian right news television channel. Although Ambassador Peck, as a U.S. diplomat, had great knowledge and experience in America's actions abroad, the news hosts were very defensive and dismissive in their interview. Wright pointed out the implications of this interview of the diplomat and gave a history of why the Ambassador was correct in his assessment. Wright began to describe America's history of terrorism with a level of detail, that Ambassador Peck did not address. The reverend outlined American terrorism in the form of its thievery of American native lands in the establishment of the country, the thievery of Africa through the transatlantic slave trade, enslaving Africans and terrorizing them in order to keep them as slaves. Wright further pointed out America's military terrorism in the form of bombing men, women in children in Grenada and Panama under the Ronald Reagan presidency. Wright added to his list of American terrorism by referencing the bombing of Qadhafi's home and family, the bombing of a pharmaceutical plant in Sudan as a means of revenge, the atomic bombing of Hiroshima and Nagasaki. Dr. Wright proclaimed in his sermon that the U.S. has through its bombing of Japan, that far more were killed than those in New York and Washington on September 11, 2001. Dr. Jeremiah Wright, before declaring "God Damn America," concludes this point of his sermon by stating what is theologically correct.

> *We have supported state terrorism against the Palestinians and Black South Africans and now we are indignant because the stuff we have done overseas is now brought right back to our own front yards. Violence begets violence.*

Hatred begets hatred. And terrorism begets terrorism. A white ambassador said that...not a black militant. The Lord showed me that this is a time for self-examination (Wright, 2003).

In the aftermath of the terrorist attacks, many American television programming would promote patriotic themes and the singing of the anthem, *America, America, God shed his grace on thee, and crown they good with brotherhood from sea to shining sea.* Wright pointed out why prophetically speaking God could not bless America while America is guilty of so much war and genocide, and its self-justification of its history. He preached that those actions of America would cause it to be damned. Wright called for self-examination for America to escape the damnation of God upon the land. Wright believed that the terrorist attacks were a sign of that damnation. Rather than celebrating the imagined goodness of America and demonizing others, America should be fearful of its own actions and accountability to God. America's image of itself is delusive and its false image of others is consistently damning and dehumanizing. It is this self-image and its dehumanizing fear of others that causes the U.S. to perpetuate its cycle of violence upon others and its minority population. It is important for White American Christianity to find ways to understand others, connect with their shared humanity, and honor their dignity, rather than viewing others as a threat to their own culture and humanity. One's own dignity and significance should not rely upon the indignity of others.

2.3 Fear as a Driving Factor of Extreme Nativism and Anti-Immigration Sentiments

Negative propaganda and demonization of the other only adds to the fears that exist between tribes, religious sects, nations, and peoples. Many corrupt leaders who have oppressed people and have started wars have identified these fears and have used them to their advantage. They often create an atmosphere where other ideas and values will not be listened to except their own; they infuse into their societies an "us against the world" mindset. This is often viewed by the outsiders as brainwashing and manipulation and is not often detected or challenged within that society. One's cultural norms, nationalism, religion, love of political power and patriotism should never be respected nor dignified above and beyond one's love for Christ's redeemed humanity. Love for humanity, which Christian anthropology suggests, bear the image of God should always be placed above love for country and its national borders.

> *In the battle against evil, especially against the evil in one's own culture, evangelical personality needs ecumenical community. In the struggle against the Nazi regime, the Barmen Declaration called the churches to reject all "other lords"—the racist state and its ideology—and give allegiance to Jesus Christ alone "who is the one Word of God which we have to hear and which we have to trust and obey in life and death." The call is as important today as it was then (Volf 2010: 93).*

Christian nationalism is one the driving factors of xenophobia on the part American religion, which resists cultures which they perceive may pose a threat to its ideals. What is lost in Christian nationalism is that no single community of Christians have a monopoly on the faith. One who is unfamiliar with American political-religious culture, may ask the question, "What is Christian Nationalism?" It is a philosophy advocating that the United States has been appointed by God to be a Christian nation from a white protestant perspective, and that it must be defended politically and possibly violently. Kristin Kobes Du Mez, a professor of history at Calvin University states these facts and further add that Christian nationalism is linked to the following:

> *Christian nationalism—intolerance toward immigrants, racial minorities, and non-Christians. It is linked to opposition to gay rights and gun control, to support for harsher punishments for criminals, to justifications for the use of excessive force against black Americans in law enforcement situations, and to traditionalist gender ideology. (Du Mez 2020: 9)*

One might also add that Christian nationalists often view ex-president Donald Trump as somewhat of *a savior* of a Christian

U.SA., who was appointed God as its defender (ibid., 8). The first violent attack on the U.S. capitol since 1812, came after the election loss of Donald Trump in November 2020, brought about by his supporters. They were angry at the election loss and feared, metaphorically speaking, that America would go to hell without him in power. They sought to violently stop the certification of votes and threatened to hang the Vice President and members of Congress. During the raid on the U.S. capitol on January 6, 2021, many rioters were holding up posters with the words "Jesus Saves." This is a picture of Christian Nationalism and what they are willing to do to save America from people are not like them.

What Christian nationalism overlooks is that the Christian faith is a world religion, and from a Christological standpoint it is the universal body of Christ. It does not belong to the United States. The idea that God favors one particular "Christian nation" above others undermines the theological view that we are all one in Christ. God is not a respecter of persons or nations. This is one of the weaknesses of protestant independence, which give strong argument in favor of Orthodoxy and Catholicity. Christian theologians should not overestimate how one's culture, national history and political reality shapes how one views and expresses their own theology. This requires humility on the part of Christians from wealthy nations. It demands that western theologians should seek out and understand the views of Christian theologian from the developing world. It may be that Christians from poorer countries may have a better grasp of the implications of basic Christology that those from the western world. This would be due to their familiarity to poverty, suffering, persecution and exploitation, and Christ's work among this class. Christian nationalism often fails to give voice to suffering and are content to remain in their own nationalistic bubble of prosperity without consideration of others. This what Emmanuel Katongole was referencing when he considered the words of Cardinal Roger Etchegaray, who was the president of the Pontifical Council for Justice and Peace, who questioned whether the blood of tribalism was more important than the waters of baptism. Katongole presented the following challenge to the global body of Christ. He utilized the Rwandan genocide to illustrate the character that the world might reflect should the blood of ethnic or national superiority run deeper. He questioned the problematic rationale behind fearing "the other." *This is the challenge. This is what the Rwandan genocide exposes for the global church to recognize. Christian expression throughout the world has too easily allowed the blood of tribalism to flow deeper than the waters of baptism (Katongole 2009: 13).*

Viewing theology through a nationalistic lens makes the blood of nationalism more important than the waters of baptism in the U.S. Most of those who are seeking asylum at the Mexican border are baptized Christians. Most black Americans who are the victims of economic marginalization and police targeting are Christians or are from Christian families. This is harmful and detrimental to the peace of the world and to the body of Christ. For example, U.S. Christians often express fear that America is losing its Christian identity, while they are simultaneously politically engaged in barring Mexicans from crossing the border or deporting them. They fail to realize that those who they fear from an immigration standpoint would indeed increase the population of Christians within America. Most Mexican and South American immigrants are devoted Catholics and would be sympathetic toward their concerns. Narrow nationalistic views and political positions are counterproductive to the Christian message. The combination of Christian nationalism and xenophobia is to a certain degree religiously suicidal.

The problem of Christian nationalism is that politics, culture and patriotism will become so strong, that the voice of Christ in the world will be drowned out. The stronger Christian nationalism grows, the body of Christ will be viewed more as a xenophobic political tribe than the spiritual and dynamic force for good in the world that Christ designed. This is the view of Croatian theologian Miroslav Volf of Yale University. He expands upon this understanding and the dangerous hunger for communal survival and its consequences. Volf calls upon the Christians in America to see themselves and their future beyond their own culture and seek to understand the way of God and the future through the lens of Christians of other nations tribes and languages.

> *The images of communal survival and flourishing our culture feeds us all too easily blur our vision of God's new creation—America is a Christian nation, we then think, for instance, and democracy is the only truly Christian political arrangement. Unaware that our culture has subverted our faith, we lose a place from which to judge our own culture. In order to keep our allegiance to Jesus Christ pure, we need to nurture commitment to the multicultural community of Christian churches (Volf 2010: 95).*

Much of the anti-immigration moods that have swept through developing countries throughout history have been based upon that fear of the other. The impression is given that the outsiders are creating chaos by bringing in different cultures and ideas, and that the new leader is committed to protecting their nation from this chaos. Efforts are put forth oftentimes through radio, television, and the internet to demonize the immigrant population or the potential immigrant population as a threat to societal order and to its resources. It is quite ironic that in a supposedly Christian society, there is a failure to understand that the God of scripture values the lives of the foreigner as much as the native. Xenophobia, according to Professor Willimon is too often blamed on a lack of education by the populace or cultural insensitivity, when it is a moral sin and evil. It is characterized as thus because of the many crimes against humanity which are symptomatic of this inner human evil.

> *Xenophobic, exclusionary fear of the Other is more than a matter of preference for people whom we enjoy hanging out with, or those with whom we feel most comfortable. In deep fear of the Other, we separate ourselves from others in order to better oppress, exploit, expulse, confine, hurt, or deny justice and access to others whom we have judged to be so Other as to be beyond the bounds of having any bond between us or any claim upon us (Willimon 2016: 14-15).*

If Christians are to be consistent with the Christological paradigm and its demands, they must acknowledge and confess how much cultural background and propaganda has shaped how they view the world. One must seek to educate oneself about the challenges and value systems of other cultures and understand how they too are viewed by others. Additionally, one must also acknowledge the sinfulness of xenophobia, and make continual efforts to battle against it both in one's own mind as well as in the community at large. Such thinking and behavior may be viewed as a normative and acceptable fear, but from a Christological standpoint, it should be viewed as a sinful condition that demands repentance. Background and upbringing are not an excuse for such fears and resistance of other cultures, because there are so many from the same culture who do not share such attitudes. Professor, American bishop, and theologian William Willimon courageously confessed how important it was for him to confess his own sin of xenophobia, and how its normalization within one's culture cannot be used to justify such attitudes. Overcoming the inclination of xenophobia, he recognized it was an ongoing process.

> *I have treated another person not in the way of Jesus, as my neighbor, but as the fearful, threatening Other. Though I have sometimes tried to excuse my sin as "just the way I was brought up" or due to my psychological insecurities, my behavior was in clear rebellion against the expectations of Christ. Yet I also write as one who, solely by the grace of God, is being redeemed of my own sinful inclination to xenophobia (Willimon 2016: 10).*

It is in this setting that the fear of cultural chaos that oftentimes leads to the rise of an authoritarian figure who will protect that society and maintain order; the natural inclination of that society is to give in to that inner fear and rally behind such leaders. The United States Constitution says that "we are endowed by our creator with certain unalienable rights." In times of crisis, citizens so often out of fear, willingly lay down such inherent rights, and give authority to an all-powerful government.

When nations feel threatened by certain ethnic groups due to a past event in history, the tendency is to fear the entire group and deny them their human dignity. An example of this may be found in the events following United States of America following the terrorist attacks in New York City and Washington DC on September 11, 2001. Additional powers to engage in military conflicts in the Middle East and Asia in order to defend against terrorism were also given. Such an act would have never passed in a time of peace and security; it was the fear of future terrorist attacks that gave the U.S. federal government unprecedented and unlimited power. All five fears were on display in the United States of America currently:

1. America became afraid of "the other," Muslims and Middle Easterners to be exact, and the U.S. president Donald Trump's attempt at a Muslim travel ban shows that this fear still exists fifteen years after "nine-eleven." This fear of "the other" was on display with U.S. President George Bush's speech to congress and the nation in which he addressed the world in stark terms, "either you are with us or against us," in the fight against foreign terrorists. Those who would not help America's military during that time would be considered enemies and should be viewed as a threat.

2. America became afraid of "chaos," that might follow future attacks and demanded more restrictive laws to be passed to maintain order

3. America became afraid of "insignificance," as a nation; they felt embarrassed and humiliated that foreign non-military persons could inflict so much pain upon them and felt the need to flex military muscle in order to maintain the respect that they felt they had. The war in Afghanistan and Iraq were waged immediately afterwards. These countries did not attack America on what is referred to as "nine-eleven."

4. America became afraid of the future. President George W. Bush and Vice President Cheney developed a doctrine of preemptive strikes. America would attack nations that

could be perceived as potential supporters of foreign terrorists as a future threat. America's war in Iraq is a primary example.

5. America became afraid of death at the hands of foreign terrorists. They feared that many more Middle Eastern terrorist were already in the country, had formed "sleeper cells," and would bring more death to its citizens. They feared that death and destruction would become commonplace if greater security measures such as more spying were not implemented. This fear even allowed room for the torture of individuals suspected of terrorism. It also changed the way air travel occurs, and more intrusive security measures were taken to avoid the hijacking and destruction of planes by foreign terrorists while traveling.

It is interesting to note that America's war in Iraq was based on the suspicion and fear that Iraq's president, Sadaam Hussein had a hidden stockpile of "weapons of mass destruction." It was also suggested that Iraqi scientists were in the beginning stages of discovering how to make a nuclear weapon and had secured the necessary chemical ingredients to do so. Vice President Dick Cheney, in the lead up to that war, would often announce their evidence of indirect links of Hussein to shadowy non-governmental militant Middle Easterners that they labeled as terrorists. Cheney even subtly suggested that Hussein may have had some links to the attacks in New York. These representations convinced most Americans to give its popular support to Bush's war in Iraq. After over four-thousand deaths of U.S. military personnel and tens of thousands of Iraqi civilian casualty deaths, it was later discovered that Hussein actually did not possess any weapons of mass destruction and had no links to the attacks in New York.

The United States government and its citizenry later learned that their fears of Iraq were unfounded. Later those United States congressmen and senators, who voted for the Iraq war, were often questioned about the new information about Hussein. Their new line of reasoning suggested that although there were no nuclear weapons in Iraq or weapons of mass destruction, the world is better off with Hussein because he was a bad actor in the world. This is an example how unfounded fear can lead to unnecessary death and destruction and conflict among nations.

This fear later led to America's intervention in the Syrian civil war, the intervention in Libya's internal conflict and the assassination attack on Libya's Colonel Quadaffi, and stronger threats and stances against the Iranians. Again, myths about America's Christian character began to emerge in the political and cultural discourse. Ideas about preemptively protecting "God's country" against Muslim terrorists who they believed intended to eliminate America's freedom and Islamicize the nation and the world.

> *God kept surfacing in the arguments for and against the war. Underneath and interpenetrating much of the concern for safety and international order were claims about God and God's relation to the United States and God's role in its future. Notable voices of American Christianity engaged important political and theological questions...President Bush identified Iraq, Iran and North Korea as an Axis of Evil that threatened the United States (Morrissey 2018: 14).*

When weapons of mass destruction were never discovered in Iraq, and that there was no connection between Saddam Hussein and September 11, 2001, terrorist attacks, the American political class justified the war in Iraq as a humanitarian liberation of Iraq from a brutal dictator and an opportunity to extend American democratic values to that part of the Middle East. The irony of this regime change campaign in Iraq is that it led to an electoral process that ushered in an Iranian backed government under Shiite influence. This process led to political instability and religious strife and the unintended consequence of Christian churches being bombed, which should have been understood by American Christians to be a part of the family of Christ. The philosophy that suggests that military conquest is justified for the purposes of spreading "Christian" values to presumably "uncivilized" nations is not a new concept. Such ideas have their foundation in the conquest narratives of the Old Testament but are antithetical and counter to the "Word of God" as revealed Christologically. Such theology gained ground in the European Middle Ages.

> *The theology of Genessi Sepulvedae (Juan Gin6s de Sepulveda) is representative of the argument justifying war against the Indians as a prerequisite for their future evangelization. Sepulveda was born in Spain c. 1490 and finished his treatise in 1545 but was forbidden to publish it. His theology is significant for many reasons, but principally because of the manner in which he managed to subordinate the imperatives of the Christian Gospel to the political and ideological actuality of the conquest (Prior 1997: 41).*

However not all U.S. Christians agree with American notions of self-defense and national exceptionalism under God. There was a minority view among more progressive thinking theologians. There were those who protested the U.S. government's propaganda concerning the need to invade Iraq and the push by white evangelicals to launch such an invasion. Bishop John Chane of the Episcopal church argued publicly against the U.S. effort, supported by Evangelicals to send a shock and awe military campaign to protect God's country and to instill fear in the Muslim population of the Middle East. Those who publicly campaigned against the war in Iraq, were labeled as terrorist sympathizers and unpatriotic. President George W. Bush, president and a white American evangelical saw himself as divinely called to the office of president and this war effort was a part of defending America against an "axis of Evil. Voices such as Bishop Chane were drowned out with calls for patriotism and the fear of another terrorist attack from Middle Easterners.

> *Bishop Chane imagines a very different relationship between God and America. In this vision of Bishop Chane, God is not involved in the same project of bringing freedom to the world. God and America are not unified in the same basic project. Instead, in Chane's rendering, God and*

> *America are in tension. God is not pleased by the nation's plans to initiate hostilities with Iraq. Indeed, according to Chane, God is opposed to America's war plans (Morrissey 2018: 17-18).*

America's reaction to the September 11, 2001, terrorist attacks failed to analyze why there is so much hostility toward the U.S. government in the Muslim world. The hyper-patriotic attitudes that America is so much a force for good in the world that it should never be blamed for anything she suffers as a result of her attitude toward foreigners. This mindset presents an obstacle to peace and discourages public debate upon such matters. Moreover, in the aftermath of those attacks the American public began to look at the Muslim world with a greater level of suspicion. Islamophobic attitudes began to increase among the Christian political right, which perhaps unknowingly, ran contrary to the Christological claims of Jesus. Bishop William Willimon reminds western theologians that Christ was all about inclusion and consistently tore down the walls of exclusion.

> *Where we expected judgment and exclusion, he enacted mercy and embrace. Where we craved unconditional affirmation of our righteousness and insider status, he slammed us with judgment upon our presumption and a call to even higher righteousness (Willimon 2016: 16-17).*

No nation is free from sin nor above analyzing what role one has played in creating so much anger and hostility in the world. If a nation is truly strong, it should be strong enough to see the good and the bad in its character without fear of being diminished. Such national arrogance is foolhardy and self-defeating. The Reverend Jeremiah Wright's call would never be heeded while such national arrogance was maintained in the aftermath of September 11, 2001. As a result, few questions were asked in this regard, particularly among those within the political Christian right in the U.S. Jeremiah Wright's September 11th sermon response was a call to war against America's own moral evils, rather against the weak and defenseless. Dr. Wright preached that America is an arrogant and racist bully on the world stage and that it needed repentance and redirect its anger against the moral evils of which it was guilty. He called upon the government, and its citizenry to launch a moral war against the evils of racism, injustice, greed, disease, inferior quality education and a for-profit health care system.

> *We have got to change the way we have been doing things as a country. We have got to change the way we have been doing things as an arrogant, racist, military superpower...Maybe we need to declare war on injustice. Maybe we need to declare war on greed. Maybe we need to declare war on the health care system that leaves the nation's poor with no health coverage. This is a time for social transformation. (Wright, 2003).*

Sadly, Dr. Wright became labeled as an unpatriotic enemy of America by the public. Moreover, due to the political winds, soon-to-be president Barack Obama was forced to remove his membership from the Trinity United Church of Christ and denounce Reverend Wright as his pastor. In order to become president, Obama could not be perceived as a black man who is angry at America and associated with the so-called militant views of justice and human rights. It is always easier to demonize those who cry out against nationalism, human rights abuses, and war crimes, than to address the problems of racism and xenophobia. Self-examination by powerful nations is difficult but urgently needed for the good of the entire human family. It is an indispensable necessity. As it relates to those who profess to embrace the Christian message, it is a Christological expectation.

There may be old wounds, old battles, dehumanizing words and centuries of bloodshed, but it is a sign of strength of character to repent, atone for the past and try to learn about the enemy's concerns, fears and aspirations. This sign of the strength of humanity is taught in what Dr. King suggested, which is *know his* (our perceived enemies) *assessment of ourselves.* One must be able to have the emotional maturity to honestly accept that assessment, without anger or verbal retaliation. When that emotional maturity is achieved, there is hope for the world. If this one principle is observed within the world's societies, it will transition the world from what Dr. Martin Luther King, Jr., described as a *thing-oriented society to a person-oriented society.*

2.4 Fear as a Driving Force for Genocide During Times of Civil Unrest

When analyzing the human emotions surrounding civil unrest, here are not many fear-based conflicts that have been as devastating as the Rwandan genocide. Susan Cook, in the introduction of her scholarly volume, *Genocide in Rwanda and Cambodia,* talks about her findings after she studied up close the causes of this conflict.

> *[After] ten years of genocide studies at Yale, she writes about the reign of Habyarimana from 1973-1994 in her anthology, and references what she believes to be the foundation of the Rwanda genocide. She makes a special note about his rhetoric, his policies and the aftermath of the 1991-1992 Rwandan civil war (Cook 2004: Description).*

She goes on to describe the cultural make-up of Rwandan society, the relationship between the Hutus and Tutsis, the problem of classicism, the problems that arose out of the civil war that was fought, and what drove the massacres. She demonstrates how the "fear of the other" and the "fear of death" took root in the midst of that civil war. The Tutsis were labeled as "enemies of the revolution." Notice how she describes the developments that lead to the genocide.

> *Habyarimana wanted Rwanda to be an agricultural society. He glorified the peasantry and pictured himself as a peasant. In his ideology of rural romanticism only the Hutu were the real peasants of Rwanda; the Tutsi were the feudal class closely associated with colonialist occupation (ibid, 3-4).*

When compared to gang violence, family break-ups, civil war and wars between nations, genocide is perhaps the ugliest and most dehumanizing form of violence. Straus defines genocide in his volume along with the psychology that produces it. It is easy to assume that genocide can only happen in an environment where people are accustomed to bloodshed and murder and in places where people have a long history of violence. Straus sets out to disprove this notion. He shows how ordinary people, under the right circumstances would also carry out genocide in similar cases. Straus describes the genocide as a moral sickness that arises when violence and murder are normalized, and fear becomes the predominant emotion within a community.

> *Genocide is about the extraordinary human violence of a character and level that is rare, about violence that represents a mind-numbing transgression of the normal respect for human life... [and how] ordinary people came to see fellow citizens, neighbors, friends, loved ones and even children as enemies who must be killed...[It] included the participation of hundreds of thousands of individuals of whom the majority had no prior history of committing lethal violence (ibid, 16).*

The genocide of the Jewish population in Nazi Germany is a striking example of how powerful propaganda can be, and there may be those who will point to the radio and media program of the Hutu government of Rwanda as the catalyst for the genocide. Straus suggests that while this may have contributed to the massacre, this is not as important a factor as many have suggested. He also points out civil war as the primary contributor, and that the genocide would not have happened without it. Straus goes further to advance the idea that the Hutus and Tutsis were neighbors and friends when the civil war was not being waged. He also disputes the popular notion that Hutus and Tutsis shared a long history of hatred and violence toward each other.

(Ibid, 23).

What is also extremely revealing about Straus' findings is how Rwandans willingly submitted to the demands of their authority figures. This mindset goes back to the universal need for authority, order and structure during chaos. Civil war is a case of extreme chaos. As Buckingham pointed out in his theory of Universal Fear and Needs, that fear of societal breakdown and ensuing chaos often creates a vacuum for authoritarian figures. Hutu leadership followed an easily understood chain of command which flowed from the higher levels down to the local leaders. They believed that their survival depended upon following orders from top to bottom. Straus contends that the perpetrators of genocide did not belong to any criminal gang and had no real history of crime or murders. Those whom he interviewed who were involved say that there was a war, and they were simply following orders, and many ordinary people in any society would make the same calculations if faced with similar fears.

> *[This points to the] critical importance of self-protection as a mechanism that can lead to violence. Many Rwandans became perpetrators because they feared the negative consequences of disobeying...The specific nature of Rwanda's war and state mattered for the calculations Rwandans made (ibid, 28).*

Straus dispels the notion that prior to the genocide that Tutsis and Hutus had a long history of inter-tribal warfare. He showed how many among them intermarried between tribes and did not give tremendous weight to their differences. Understanding who the enemy is one of the important needs during war, and the Hutu leadership successfully classified the Tutsis as the enemy. Where there is fear of the future and chaos there is also the human need to classify things and the Hutu leader if clarification which is one of the most basic human needs.

While diminishing the role of long held animosity between the tribes, the author goes on to point out the three areas that laid the groundwork for large scale indiscriminate killing in the tens of thousands. Those who did not want to kill their Tutsi neighbors feared the consequences of not obeying the orders to kill. He also demonstrates how authoritarian minded rulers took advantage of these fears not merely to protect the country, but to keep themselves in power and to maintain their place in Rwandan society.

> *Rather than preexisting ethnic antipathy, rather the principal mechanisms, I argue were (1) wartime*

uncertainty and fear (2) social pressure (3) opportunity in the aggregate, Hutus killed because they wanted to protect themselves during a war and during a period of intense uncertainty because they felt that complying with those who told them to kill would be less costly than not complying... (ibid, 25).

It is also pointed out that the hardliners were perhaps more fearful of no longer being in power than fear of the Tutsis dominating the nation. This human fear of insignificance among Hutu leadership reached a destructive and desperate level in the case of the Rwandan genocide. They felt that if they did not order a massive level of killing and inflict as much pain as possible that they would go down in history as a defeated group and perhaps executed by their enemies.

The more the hardliners felt that they were losing power and the more they felt their enemy was not playing by the rules, the more the hardliners radicalized. After the president was assassinated and the rebels began advancing, the hardliners let loose. They chose genocide as an extreme, vengeful and desperate strategy to win a war they were losing (Ibid, 28).

One of the larger questions that is often asked of contemporary western leaders who were in power is "Why didn't you intervene when you saw the genocide in Rwanda was about to begin?" Straus points out that indeed an intervention would have satisfied the need for order, certainty authority among the Hutu population. Straus also shows how the fear was so extreme, and the killing was so quick and widespread, that no nation would have been able to respond swiftly enough.

An outside intervention would have changed the dynamics for a number of reasons. An intervention would have stabilized Rwanda. Stabilization would have short-circuited the uncertainty and fear that drove the violence and underpinned the hardliners ability to carry the day (Ibid, 28).

One of the arguments often used is "These people have been fighting forever." - Not only is this historically inaccurate, but it frames the issue as something unsolvable and intractable. It also reinforces ideas of Africans as barbaric and inherently violent. It dehumanizing and inconsistent with theological anthropology, which identifies all races as created in the image of God. It is this image of God in humanity, that makes Christian eschatology meaningful. It is this eschatological theology of the image of God in humanity that makes all persons equally valuable and worthy of the redemption that was achieved at Calvary. However, it is the historical denial of the humanity of the African race, which seemingly gives license for European Christians to turn a blind eye to such genocidal actions. This faulty view of black humanity allows the European to blame such a mass killing crusade on the so-called subhuman and barbaric nature of Africans for such an atrocity. Emmanuel Katongole, a renown African Catholic theologian who served as associate professor of Theology at Duke University, agrees through the following experience as he has studied the Rwandan genocide. He connects the catastrophe to the dehumanizing perspectives of Africans by Christian missionaries and theologians.

> *The portrayal of the wastage of lives in Africa as "tribal" violence seems to carry with it a certain degree of acceptability—and indeed expectation in the West...I was also beginning to see theologically that a new claim regarding African lives is being announced and enacted: namely, that these are not unique, precious, sacred lives; these are Africans, mere bodies to be used, mere masses to be exploited (Katongole 2011: xxx).*

A true Christian anthropology would view Africans as part of the same family of humanity, rather than the barbaric "other" which needs being civilized and saved from its cultural backwardness. It is those nation states who have plundered the world's resources at the expense of human flourishing and familyhood who need "saving." Perhaps a mature view of the familyhood of the human race would have prompted Europeans to intervene to assist in delivering the Rwandans.

> *Of course, each of those bodies is precious to God. Each bears the very image of God. But we cannot begin to understand the life and death of these bodies until we consider another body—the body politic. (Katongole 2009: 7)*

This body politic involves both the domestic as well as the international body politic. Both bodies have historically devalued the bodies of Africans through slavery, colonialism and Eurocentric miseducation. It is better to re-orient and transform the body politic than sacrifice those bodies which Christ values above all. The fact that those deaths occurred in the hundreds of thousands, such a statistic can easily overlook the individual and familial nature of the suffering.

Another excuse offered by U.S. diplomats for not intervening militarily to try to end the genocide, is that such an intervention was not in the national security interest of the nation. It interesting to note that in late 1991 and early 1992, the U.S. government intervened militarily to rescue the Kuwaiti nation, from occupation by the Iraqi government. Both Kuwait and Iraq are known for their vast treasury of oil. The economy of the U.S. and the West are extremely dependent on fossil fuels. The leader of the Iraqi government, Saddam Hussein also had his sights on oil rich Saudi Arabia. The U.S. could not stand by, and watch Hussein carry out his ambitions. It was too great of a risk for oil dependent nations. It seems obvious to any casual observer, that had Rwanda been an oil rich country upon whom the west depended. There likely would have been a swift intervention militarily. Where were the voice of the American right and its Christian political base during this time? Where were their voices? Due to national and ethnic differences between Africa and the west, it was easy to view the genocide as the problem of others, rather than a problem of humanity. It seemed as if Rwanda was left to perish during the genocide because they did not have as much to offer as Kuwait or Saudi Arabia. However, they had something far greater to offer, which is their dignified humanity. All races and tribes are unique and have something significant to offer for the advancement of the human race. Katongole suggests *that the crisis of Western Christianity is reflected back to the church in the broken bodies of Rwanda.* (Katongole 2009: 8) Not only did the western church in the U.S. fail to pressure their government, but the colonial history of Rwanda was founded by European Chiristians, whose classist hierarchal structures paved the way for future violence. Professor Katongole informs readers about the political history of Rwanda and its future impact.

> *The genocide of 1994 did not erupt out of nowhere. It has a political history. It happened in a nation called Rwanda, with certain borders and laws and economic policies that had been in place for some time. The killers and the killed in Rwanda were Rwandans-which is to say, they shared a political history where the labels Hutu and Tutsi meant something, not only about who you were but also about how you were supposed to relate to those who were not like you. When Hutus were told to kill their Tutsi neighbors in 1994, they either did or they were killed. Rwanda's genocide is not just a story about the bodies of some who were victims and others who were killers. It is about the ultimate manifestation of a body politic that was sick from the time it was conceived (Ibid., 7).*

Concerning the Rwandan genocide, the U.S may not be guilty of the sin of commission but rather the sin of omission. They had the power to do good and did not. This root cause of this sin of omission lies in the denial of Rwandan humanity and failure to recognize those in that part of the world as members of the same family. Military intervention may not have been in the national security interest of the U.S., but it would have been in the security interest of the human family. When one part of the family is not valued, the entire family is threatened. What happens in one part of the world can also happen in another. While the human family was alien to God and God being alien to human race, the Creator took a risk in joining the human family through the incarnation. Christian theologians and clergymen who have proximity to state power, instead of encouraging displays of power, should encourage the state to take similar risks by making themselves vulnerable in their outreach to others who they view as threatening. Methodist theologian William Willimon draws the connection through the theology of the incarnation and reconciliation.

> *That God has enabled us to know God not as a threatening, vague, distant Other but as a vulnerable, intimate friend is at the heart of the good news about God. The cross is not only revelation but also vocation. God continues to take great risk (Phil 2) in reaching out to us, refusing to save the world without us. Jesus Christ is not only God helping us but also God's incredible vulnerability in summoning us to help God's work of reconciliation (2 Cor 5:18) (Willimon 2016: 17).*

Would it have been risky for foreign nations with power to intervene? It would have, but according to Willimon, God also took a risk in reaching out to humanity in Christ. Instead of turning a deaf ear to the cries of suffering Rwandans during those one-hundred days, the Christian community in the Western world should have been foremost in crying out for the deliverance of a valuable section of the human family. Such an intervention might have been risky but love for humanity is worth the risk. William Willimon draws commentary from a Christological perspective. He suggests that humans were all alien and foreign to God, yet Christ intervened to deliver. Should not one manifest the same level of risky compassion for those who are not part of our history, culture, or ethnicity, that God has shown the human family in Christ?

Emmanuel Katongole declares from his findings that the body politic in Rwanda, with its history of colonial manipulation, that fueled the flames for the genocide. Katongole agrees that the political and economic structure which privileged one ethnic group over another set the stage for the atrocity. The fact that the modern state of Rwanda, which was founded by White Christians, could develop such an Un Christlike and corrupt political structure is quite revealing.

> *If we are to take seriously the political history that led to 1994, I must also say as a Christian writing to fellow Christians that this is a story about another body—the broken body of Christ. The history of Rwanda's body*

> *politic is one undeniably shaped by Christian missions. If ever there were a "Christian nation," Rwanda was it... (Katongole 2009: 8).*

This body politic historically benefitted their colonial "masters" and deprived the population of the familyhood that otherwise would have existed. Historically speaking, the colonial structure sacralized the body politic above the bodies that Jesus redeems. Katangole argues for a society in Rwanda that demolishes structures that privileges one class or ethnicity above another. Those who are truly Christian after the order of Jesus of Nazareth should in a "Christian nation" develop a Christian identity which prioritizes the common humanity of the other above the contrived differences of colonial powers. *"The only hope for our world after Rwanda's genocide is a new kind of Christianidentity for the global body of Christ* (Katongole 2009: 8)." This new identity is the one which Christ envisioned and is the only way to repair the broken body of Christ.

This self-defeating fear of the other exemplified by Westernized Christian societies which denies familyhood and perpetuates broken bodies and spirits may look to the Markan account to be informed. The gospel of Mark refers to a chained resident in the area of Decapolis who suffered from demonic attack (which may represent the oppressive Roman legions) and social marginalization. Jesus liberated him. What is ironic about the account, according to theology professor and author Emerson B. Powery, is that those who isolated him were more afraid of him post-liberation than when he was in chains. This is true although he was liberated and "clothed and in his right mind." Powery goes on to draw the parallel of that account and the subtle fear that black advancement or the liberation of others is a threat to the social order. He cites the late civil rights leader Revd. Otis Moss in his work, who refers to the fact that most White Christians were satisfied while the enslaved and oppressed in America were chained confined to the cotton fields. They too became afraid when the chains were thrown off, and they began to leave the fields to protest and gain political advancements in the US (Powery 2007: 131). The same is true of the fear that other nations are rising up and recovering from the colonial era, while it appears that the U.S. is losing influence and power. Love does not fear when others are unshackled but celebrates their deliverance.

Dr. Eric Betts

3 LICE, LABELS, LIES

Dr. Martin Luther King Jr was not only a civil rights leader but an advocate for world peace and international cooperation. One of his famous speeches was his condemnation of the Vietnam War in 1967. The citizenry of the western world had extraordinarily little knowledge of the factual issues and struggles going on in Southeast Asia. This lack of knowledge among the populace empowered the United States government to tell the story in the way that would shine a positive light on their military ambitions. The 1950's and 1960's were a fearful time because of the controversy between the US and the communist nation called the Soviet Union. Those times were very fearful due to the geopolitical struggle between capitalism which was the foundational economic-political ideology of the United States and the communistic views of the Soviet Union. What made the struggle so fearful in the US was the idea that if the Soviet Union took over the world, all would suffer under the terrible yoke of communism. Many thought that the United States military efforts were all about preventing such a scenario and even counteracting the Soviet Union on the global stage. They felt that they were spreading the American ideals of capitalism and democracy. Even more fearful was the reality that both powers had obtained an unlimited and unrivaled nuclear arsenal aimed at defending their countries from one another or even attacking if necessary.

The United States, through media and other propaganda, had the ability to label as "communist," nations or political movements, who were not communists. They were labeled as such because they challenged their interests on the global stage. Nonetheless, Americans who trusted their government, were influenced by such propaganda, and therefore supported their military interventionism abroad. Those who opposed America's military efforts in Vietnam were labeled as siding with the communists who the US public viewed as evil and atheistic. Daniel Kirkpatrick, a Research Fellow with the Conflict Analysis Research Centre, University of Kent, UK identifies how labels are so effective in propaganda campaigns around the world and hinders the publics ability to hear other views or to hear the views or the cries of the opposing side.

> *The freedom to express one's opinions, even if we disagree with them is widely recognized as a central pillar of democracy...And yet there is a disturbing trend taking place whereby certain views are being increasingly labeled extremist, terrorist, far right, or communist. Rather than engage with the assumptions or arguments such categories represent. These labels are used to categorically dismiss debate (Kirkpatrick 2019: 14).*

Millions in the western world were unaware of the political dynamics occurring in South Asia, but it was enough for them to know that America was fighting a just war against communism, and that they were keeping it from spreading into Asia and other parts of the world. Hundreds of thousands of American troops lost their lives not utterly understanding the reasons why there was ever a conflict in Asia; but were sufficiently aware that they were fighting for American interests. Honesty is critical when it comes to resolving world conflict. A nation should be honest with themselves and those who have competing interests. The United States government was not honest in portraying the struggle in Asia as a battle between communism and people trying to free themselves from it. The public was not aware that it was actually a struggle between European colonialism and a desire for those who suffered under that colonialism to break free and take charge of their destiny.

In King's view, the US should have sided with that independence movement rather than helping the French to put it down. Dehumanizing labels were a very potent weapon in the hands of the American government to shape the conversation about geopolitics in a way that benefited them. Dr. King, in his 1967 Riverside Church speech, sought to expose to the American public the factual issues, and that it had nothing to do with communism's spread. He exposed America's attempt to label the liberation movement in unflattering terms so that there would be no sympathy for them, that their cries would not be heard, and that they may gain unwavering support for America's efforts.

> *Perhaps a more difficult but no less necessary task is to speak for those who have been designated as our enemies. What of the National Liberation Front, that strangely anonymous group we call "VC" or "communists"? ...How do they judge us when our officials know that their membership is less than twenty-five percent communist, and yet insist on giving them the blanket name (King 1967: Sermon at Riverside Church, New York)?*

Another way in which nations can expand their power is to dehumanize their opponent by labeling them as violent terrorists. In the case of the Palestinian struggle, this label has also proven to be extremely effective in maintain the presence of the United States and Europe in the Arab world. Most westerners are unaware of the struggle of the Palestinian people and are never encouraged to "walk a mile in their moccasins." Unwavering defense against the state of Israel against "Palestinian terrorism" is the popular view due to how western politicians and western news outlets have chosen to characterize the middle east struggle. The label of terrorist is often used to dehumanize and remove any sympathy toward Palestinians in the Western world.

> *They (the Israelis) teach their soldiers to understand that you are not really human, that they can do whatever they want with you, since what is really desired is your disappearance. We must really ask, as humans, what is to be done about this hunger for more, this greed that is self-blinding (Makdisi 2010: 18, 21).*

One of the primary reasons given for America's unbreakable and uncritical support of Israel's militarism is that it is their closest ally and only democracy in the Middle East. It would be extremely difficult to find a question posed by any western journalist, such as "How can a state be both an occupying power and a democracy at the same time?" When the light is truly shed upon the daily suffering of the Palestinian people, those who see the truth of the matter are shocked and amazed. Such was the case with Alice

Walker, an African American novelist, short story writer, poet, and social activist, upon reading about their struggle.

When Alex Walker began to read first-hand reports about the Palestinian struggle, she immediately identified with their experience. She compared the Palestinian's oppression to the suffering that Black Americans suffered under the Jim Crow laws of the American South. Her commentary shows what happens when geopolitics and propaganda are set aside for the common good. What results can be very eye-opening and heart wrenching. It is then that the day-to-day human injustices and painful experiences are revealed. These revelations have the potential to draw from the well of human compassion that otherwise would not exist. Those in power who desire to shape certain geopolitical narratives are often determined to keep the human stories from the public and focus almost entirely on geopolitics. Walker was shocked when learning about how the Palestinians were being treated by the Israeli government and was concerned that such policies were supported by United States taxpayers.

> *It brought up too many memories of being black and living in the United States under American-style apartheid. The daily insults to one's sense of being human... Why didn't someone tell me! I was blissfully happy without such knowledge! And then too: I didn't realize I was paying—with my taxes (over a trillion dollars since 1948)—for so much suffering in a part of the world I never think about (Makdisi 2010: 18-21)!*

Having examined the plight of Palestinians in the Middle East, Walker concludes that such suffering will never end until one important dynamic is achieved. She points out how so much of the suffering takes place outside of the view of most of humanity because it so often fails to make into the large world media outlets. These media outlets choose what they see as the best stories to cover. There is perhaps no greater example of this than the way the state of Israel has illegally taken possession of Palestinian agricultural lands in order to create roads and erect walls, and the suffering that follows.

They [the global media] also have major corporate interests as it relates to those who advertise during their programs, those who own them and make investments in them. It is also the case that conflict, and conquest is profitable for many of the major world corporations due to the equipment and services they provide. Walker declares that the oppression and pain that Palestinians experience must be highlighted. It is believed that such revelations would appeal to our common humanity. She explains why this is a major obstacle in solving one of the world's longest conflicts and how the masses have the potential for compassion if given the opportunity to see for themselves.

> *This will require enormous belief in us as children of this paradise, otherwise known as Earth. That we do, in fact, belong here, and have a right to be here, unmolested and protected in our homes, churches, mosques, and schools. We are designed, I believe, us human beings, to instinctively wish to protect and cherish each other (Ibid, 22).*

Walker amazingly and beautifully points out that humans are not designed by their creator to be cruel and coldhearted toward those who are from diverse backgrounds. Even though this world is filled with greed, murder, theft and meanness, Walker has faith that humanity can indeed discover its inner higher angels, if given the chance to set aside politics and observe suffering for themselves, that they can indeed make a difference. This belief of hers, that the real instinct of humans is to reach out a hand of help to each other versus destroying each other, is a profound, and hopeful observation. Should Walker's idealism become a reality, the world would certainly have the potential to free itself from its worst version of itself. Humanity functions at its best, according to Walker, when all people's groups treat one another with dignity as they themselves desire to be treated with dignity. She unlocks the reason this principle is so important.

> *The reason the scripture says, 'Do unto others as you would have them do unto you,' is because our species, like other creatures in nature, learn our behavior from each*

> *other...If the behavior that we use is abusive, violent, and cruel, then that is the behavior that will eventually come around again to us. That is why the world is encircled with wars small and large, and why so many humans are mistaken in the belief that they can be happy having raped, pillaged, murdered, or destroyed someone else (ibid., 21).*

In other words, when human beings continue to lower the standard of what is acceptable in their interactions with one another, will in turn suffer the consequences of that low standard. It is time to raise the standard of what is acceptable, not only for the good of others, but for the happiness of one's own tribe. The futility of preserving one's own tribe, culture and society through dehumanizing practices and violence is not always obvious to the perpetrators, but consequently deprives them of the harmonious existence they might otherwise enjoy. The purpose of divinely given (because they reflect heaven's values of human dignity and the principle of doing to others what one would desire to be done to oneself) international human rights laws is that the nations of the world may set standards of what are shared standards of what it means to be human, and to participate with mutual appreciation for one another's humanness as members of the human family. It is when those standards are violated as in the case of the Palestinian/Israeli conflict that chaos ensues. Ali Abunimah is a noted Palestinian journalist and advocate of a one-state solution, which involves Israelis and Palestinians living together as citizens of a single nation. He explains in a practical sense how mutual standards of acceptability function in a world where everyone's humanity is reverenced. Palestinian terrorism is understood as unacceptable, but Israeli terrorism, which violates international laws to which they have agreed, are often excused, or overlooked. It may be argued that the Israeli government is permitted to act in inhumane ways because they are a great military power, a wealthy nation and have the backing of the powerful Western nations. However, wealth and power does not eradicate the universally accepted principle of "do unto others as you would have it done unto you." Our humanity is not defined by wealth of power but by our Creator's design and purpose. Displacement, occupation, and dispossession are enemies to the basic ideals of human existence that all seek to enjoy. Ali Abunimah points out that there are no different standards of acceptable human behavior because one happens to be a security officer or soldier of the Israeli government.

> *It is unacceptable for a Palestinian to draw on his history of oppression and suffering to justify harming innocent Israeli citizens. It is equally unacceptable for an Israeli to invoke his belief in an ancient covenant between God and Abraham to justify bulldozing the home and seizing the land of a Palestinian farmer (Abunimah 2007: 18).*

Palestinian suffering is real and unacceptable, but it does not occur because they do not have a voice on the international stage. They most certainly do. The Palestinians could appeal to the United Nations, as they have representatives who are sent there to speak to their issues. They can appeal to world leaders based on the agreements of the Geneva Conventions. The UN (United Nations), Amnesty International and other human rights organizations have condemned Israel's subjugation and cruelty toward the Palestinian people, but none seem to have the power to eradicate the problem. Therefore, such condemnations are meaningless as it relates to the Palestinian's future. The fact that these international peace organizations have little power to act upon these violations, affirms the beliefs of the militant Palestinians who declare that they have no voice on the world stage. They feel that conflict is their only hope. Israel appears to be untouchable due to the support it receives from the Western powers and its media empire. Israel agrees in writing with the language of the Geneva Convention, while simultaneously undermining its principles in its policy toward the Palestinians. This is strikingly remarkably and embarrassingly contradictory. Almost every prohibition outlined in the Fourth Geneva Convention, Israel is in violation in its treatment of the Palestinians.

> *The Fourth Geneva Convention of 1949, to which Israel is a signatory, spells out precisely what an occupying power can and cannot do. "Outrages upon personal dignity; extrajudicial executions; torture; violence to life and*

> *transfers of population; settlement and colonization; the wanton destruction of private or public property; collective punishment—these are all specifically forbidden by the Convention* (Makdisi 2010: 37).

The restrictions which are forced upon the Palestinians by the Israeli government, are strikingly familiar. They are harsh reminders of the cruelty and ruthlessness of the apartheid regime of South Africa, yet western leaders ignore this reality. One exception, among western leaders would be former U.S. president, Jimmy Carter. Carter identified the occupation and wall-building across Palestine is indeed apartheid (Carter 2006). Archbishop Desmond Tutu also drew this comparison when he said, *some people are enraged by comparisons between the Israeli-Palestinian conflict and what happened in South Africa...Moreover, for those of us who lived through the dehumanizing horrors of the apartheid era, the comparison seems not only apt, it is also necessary. It is necessary if we are to persevere in our hope that things can change* (Ateek 2008: 7). The Palestinian people are not free, yet the very nations who support the government of Israel, claim to be the guardians of freedom and liberty around the world. The famous proverb about the need to "walk in another's moccasins," should be sought when it involves the restrictions and limitations inflicted upon the Palestinian peoples. The lack of empathy or metaphorically walking in the Palestinian shoes, has created an environment where there is more sympathy for the oppressor than the oppressed. When one considers what the Palestinian must endure in his daily life, it should create a righteous anger against those who are the cause of such pain. If the world powers have concluded in modern times that South African apartheid was inhumane, they must know or should know that Israeli apartheid is equally inhumane.

> *According to Amnesty International, there are about 5,000 Israeli military orders regulating Palestinian life in the occupied territories...This is not to mention the formidable set of permanent physical obstacles in the form of sprawling Jewish settlements, and a road network for the Jewish settlers, built on Palestinian land, to which*

Palestinians are denied access (Ibid, 35).

The Israeli government may be aware that should its own citizens ever set aside politics and become more sensitive to the human side of the issues, that this would disempower them in their efforts to persecute an entire population. To win the support of their citizenry, the Israeli government is aware that they must dehumanize the Palestinians to their population. This dehumanization campaign gives them, in their view, the moral authority to carry out the outrages which they inflict upon a people with no voice and few resources. The language that is used by the Israeli military and government would be considered racist and xenophobic in any other context. Those who dare to fight back through militia groups in order to achieve their freedom, are so often labeled as "terrorists." This places the Israeli government on a higher moral ground as far as the western governments are concerned, and the sympathy that should go to the Palestinians is received by the Israelis. This label of "terrorist" toward the Palestinians causes them to appear inhuman and evil as far as Israel's supporters are concerned. This label makes it appear that the Palestinians are deserving of all the attacks that the state of Israel directs toward them and that they alone are to blame for all the suffering they endure. Not only are those who resist labeled as "terrorists," but Israel has gone as far as create an environment where Palestinians can freely be labeled as dirty and as contaminants to be avoided.

> *The Israelis have built new roads that deliberately deviate from Palestinian communities, the Israeli army calls these "sterile" roads because they are "uncontaminated" by Palestinians. The army has cleared about 200 feet on either side of these roads Palestinians cannot build, tend, cultivate, or grow anything (Ibid, 61-62).*

Because of the hateful climate among Israeli politicians, political leaders can vent their racist views without correction. There is no fear of shame or dishonor when it comes to dehumanizing the Palestinian population. If the Palestinians are indeed violent and inhuman, then it appears that efforts to remove them from their land is justified. Who would ever want to try to understand, empathize or show compassion to a population that is considered bloodthirsty, vengeful, and identified by politicians as a 'lice' and a 'cancer' on society. There is only on alternative to removing lice or cancer and that is to cut it out and destroy it. This is exactly what the Palestinian population feels that the state of Israel desires to do to them.

> *The right-wing National Union bloc, which incorporates Moledet, currently holds nine seats in the Israeli parliament, compared with the twelve seats held by Likud, the most prominent opposition party. It does not hold any cabinet posts in the current Israeli government, but it held posts in the previous government, and the one before that. Ze'evi himself, who compared Palestinians to "lice" and "cancer," served as minister of tourism in Ariel Sharon's first government (ibid, 39-40).*

Although there are many differences between one's own culture and the many cultures of the world, there are also aspects that are held in common. The casual observer may not understand the language, customs, culture, history, and way of life of other societies which are unlike their own. One may not be able to relate to the political issues which are faced by other nation groups, but it is not difficult to relate to matters surrounding the family unit. Across all cultures, there is the need for one's children to be fed, protected, and educated. The most human part of any group will desire the safety and survival of all children in any language or population group outside of their own. It is hurtful and heart wrenching to see children suffering regardless of their background or culture.

A mother of any group can relate to a mother of any population group who is seen crying about the loss of her children or fear of dangers that threaten them. The mothers of each group are the same in this way. One of the barriers which keep nation groups from standing up and being a voice for the oppressed other, is the inability to hear the day-to-day struggles of real mothers and fathers who desire survival and a prosperous future for their children. The strict focus on geopolitics, economics, dehumanizing rhetoric, and competition for resources tends to drown out the stories which need to be heard. In the case of the Palestinian struggle, there are many stories about mothers, fathers and children that are never heard. A powerful example of that struggle is the daily battle for Palestinian mothers and fathers to safely send their children to school and securely return home again. The roadblocks, checkpoints and the sight of armored vehicles and military weaponry that Palestinian children must daily encounter should make any mother or father shudder.

> *'There have been incidents where the soldiers chased the kids, threw teargas canisters at them and yelled at them. these incidents have had serious effects on my kids. they are afraid to walk to school and often ask me to come with them. in many cases, the soldiers won't let the kids cross the road and they can't get to the school.' As a result, Abdel Karim and Suleiman frequently miss classes. sometimes the soldiers let the kids cross to school but not back home, so that they have to take an 18-mile detour all the way around the nearby Jewish settlements to get back home (Ibid, 63-64).*

This story is one of thousands which are untold. Israel claims that such restrictions and roadblocks are the fault of the Palestinian militants who retaliate violently against the occupation. The question that most political leaders and foreign nations do not consider is "What would they do if someone came and militarily occupied your homeland, your farms, your family property and has sought to dispossess your kindred from what you believe belongs to you?" If the Palestinian militants do nothing, it appears as if they are surrendering to occupation, and if they react, they are viewed as violent. Most do not ask themselves the question, "how would you feel?" Such compassion may be the beginning of justice, peace and reconciliation. Where there was once fear of the Palestinian people and their cause, such understanding and human connection may eradicate such fears and peace will be possible in the Middle East. Christian clergypersons, ecclesiastical institutions, and theologians should be at the forefront of leading the world across the bridge of fear and into a destiny of hope and reconciliation. This would be consistent with the Christological perspective of the New Testament and the self-sacrificing condescending "Word of God," who admonished his followers to love and pray for their enemies and gave his life for a human race that was alien to him. This should be the case not only in the area of Palestinian oppression, but wherever injustice and conflict may be found. The Palestinian dilemma is only one dimension of inhumanity that must be studied, such experiences have its historical precedents and present-day similarities in many parts of the world. Christian theologians should not be engaged in fearmongering against other populations, but should labour as the Apostle Paul suggested, to be examples of that *perfect love which casts out all fear, for he that feareth is not made perfect in love* (1 John 4:18).

Nadera Shalhoub-Kevorkian, who grew up in Haifa, Israel is a law professor and world renown lecturer on Palestinian issues, especially Palestinian women's issues. She is an alumnus of the Hebrew University of Jerusalem. Shalhoub-Kevorkian refers to the politics of fear and "security theology" in her lectures and writings. She references Jewish fundamentalist, backed by American Christian Zionists, as proponents of this theology of fear or security theology. She says, *Jewish fundamentalists portray Jerusalem in terms of a "sacred geography," and the fear of the violation of its sacredness through the presence of non-Jews has opened new spaces for additional uprooting of and violence against Palestinians* (Kevorkian 2015: 25).

Kevorkian analyzes the biblical claims of the Chosen people/Promised land which she states is at the *"heart of Jewish and Christian Zionism and which justify racial violence"* (Kevorkian 2015: 24). Shalhoub-Kevorkian makes clear that is a fear industry which exists to dehumanize Palestinians as a population that threatens security and the world and should be feared. She exposes the partnership between the United States and the state of Israel in driving the narrative of fear in order to further empower the state of Israel against the Palestinian population. This industry of fear, according to Shalhoub-Kevorkian, is committed being silent about non-violent efforts at peace by the Palestinian people.

> *For decades the United States has supported Israel's fear industry and its security theology, even as Israel continues to commit war crimes, grab valuable land and resources, fragment the remaining Palestinian land with additional settlements and expand settlements in Jerusalem in violation of UN Security Council edicts. Non-violent reactions by Palestinians and solidarity groups are rarely noticed...for they do not serve the fear industry, rather, Palestinian violence is always emphasized (Kevorkian 2015: 26).*

Shalhoub-Kevorkian also makes clear that the industry of fear and theology of security is another branch of racism which privileges the so-called civilized class over the so called violent and barbaric culture. *Portraying the Arab/Palestinian population in "zoological" terms—as primitive, barbaric, uncivilized and ultimately as terrorists—constitutes a deliberate and well-calculated manifestation of privileging the Jewish settler over the monstrous native* (Kevorkian 2015: 18)

Such racist ideas are not exclusive to the state of Israel. These same tactics are utilized in the United States against the black population by labeling them as fatherless, violent, and criminal and thus a threat to white spaces and property. This propaganda makes it appear that black Americans are deserving of police brutality and mass incarceration, and the denial of the assumption of innocence. However, in the case of Israel, there is an entire school of theology, advanced by Jewish fundamentalists and American evangelicals which prioritizes Israeli comfort over the humanity of Palestinians. Shalhoub-Kevorkian details the inhumane treatment of Palestinians which stems from the "security risk" branding which is unjustly placed upon them.

> *Their branding as "security risk" justifies numerous interventions into the most intimate realms of their everyday life: to delay or deny passage to pregnant women undergoing labor at checkpoints, to deny them medical*

assistance in life-threatening circumstances, to hinder family reunifications, to demolish homes and deny dead bodies the right to dignified burial. These security justifications are closely tied to fears deeply rooted in Israeli society (Kevorkian 2015: 13).

These inhumane practices inflicted upon the Palestinians are rarely highlighted or covered in the mass media in the United States. It is assumed that the Israelis are simply walking along peacefully, and suddenly violent Palestinians, without provocation, have launched a rocket into Israeli territory. This is the narrative created by mass media but rarely is the daily violence and pain of military occupation brought to the center of the discussion. Destroying homes, denying medical attention for the pregnant women in labor, destroying families, cannot be viewed as consistent with the vision of Jesus, yet many American evangelicals believe that this is what Palestinians deserve. The hunger, poverty and denial of emergency medical aid created by the many checkpoints are acts of daily violence, should never be supported by those who claim to believe in the healing and restorative ministry of Jesus. The Jesus who reconciles all people unto himself is noted as one who healed the sick and fed five thousand souls on a hillside. This Jesus presents the good Samaritan a model for all. He held up the Samaritan as an example as one who did not fear the thieves and robbers but risked his own safety to help a victimized a Jewish man on the side of the road. The theology of fear is inconsistent with the spirit of Jesus which casts out all fear. It must also be remembered the Jesus of Nazareth was victimized by state violence on the cross because he was believed to be a security threat. (John 11:50). This same spirit is perpetuated in the same geographical location where Jesus himself was crucified, and he is being re-crucified today through the Israeli security state in the person of Palestinian. As the crowds yelled "Crucify him," two-thousand years ago in Palestine, the American evangelical likewise encourages and participates in this crucifixion through their theological and political rhetoric.

4 CHRISTIAN THEOLOGY, ZIONISM, AND PALESTINIAN HUMANITY

4.1 The History of Anti-Semitism and Contemporary Israeli State Violence

In order to understand the relationship between eschatology and Christian support for the development expansion of the state of Israel, one must understand the philosophy of Zionism. What exactly is Zionism? To understand this, is to also understand Christian Zionism.

> *Zionism emerged in Europe in the middle of the nineteenth century with the defined goal of terminating the "abnormal" political situation of the Jewish diaspora, that is, statelessness of the Jews, and of creating a mode of collective life based on a national state (Amar-Dahl 2016: 5).*

Christian Zionism is similar, except that it establishes and supports a biblical mandate for the establishment and expansion of the secular state of Israel. They believe that the establishment of Israel in Palestine was divine intervention for the fulfillment of Old Testament prophecies.

In order to understand the following concepts, it must be understood that when Zionism or Christian Zionism is challenged in this thesis, it is the hardline perspective that is being criticized. Defining Zionism, Christian Zionism, and Zionism itself can prove challenging. Professor Stephen Spector, a Christian who is of Jewish ancestry, illustrates the following challenge.

> *Definitions of the term tend to be too narrow or too broad. Church of Scotland minister Walter Riggans defined a Christian Zionist very inclusively, as any Christian who supports the Zionist aim of building the state of Israel, its*

army, government, and other institutions. He added that the term could apply even more generally, to any Christian who supports Israel for any reason. Defined in that way, the phrase is so generic that it can denote, for example, liberal Protestants who sympathize with the Palestinians over the Israelis but who support the Jewish state's existence... (Spector 2008: 9).

It is for this reason that anyone Christian who supports the existence of the state of Israel might be considered a Christian Zionist. Yet everyone who believes and supports the state of Israel, would not consider themselves a Zionist. The theological Zionists addressed in this section are those who view the initial injustice of population displacement of the Palestinians for the establishment of the state of Israel as divinely mandated, who presently believe that the state of Israel has the biblical right to all of Palestine, and who disregard the suffering of the Palestinian people. Additionally, it will include those who take a militant position against Palestinian statehood and the population itself. While there are Evangelicals who are sensitive to the suffering of the plight of the Palestinians, their voices are not the loudest. It is the most vocal among the hardliners in the Evangelical community that are being critiqued.

One of the greatest obstacles to world peace and universal familyhood is the theology of a modern day divinely sanctioned state of Israel. This theological viewpoint is an assault on the common humanity of all races. When one section of humanity is downgraded and downtrodden, the whole of humanity is affected. Violence and crimes against humanity in one place gives subtle license and unintentional acceptability to inhumanity in all places. American evangelical support, which drives much of the favoritism toward the state of Israel, undermines US credibility and moral standing in other parts of the world, where it might be useful in eliminating conflict. This is the view of Palestinian theologian, Father Naim Ateek, who adds that such a militaristic position which supports violence creates an atmosphere for more violence.

The United States could contribute to the healing of the world [as Jesus did] because of its tremendous power and resources; instead, it has allowed itself to be a party to injustice and oppression...Its total identification with one side has stripped it of credibility as well as its ability to broker a peace longed for by millions of people throughout the Middle East...What is tragic about such blind support for Israel is that it not only prevents peace from coming about in Palestine and Israel, but also encourages violence throughout the Middle East. One of the main causes of Muslim resentment against the United States is America's unnatural and illogical bias against justice for the Palestinians (Ateek 2008: 44).

Additionally, the violence, occupation, and displacement of the Palestinian population by the government of Israel, diminishes human commonality. This becomes extremely problematic when such militaristic activity against an economically and militarily weaker population group has the support of a great proportion of Christian theologians.

It should also be noted that anti-Semitism has been an inhumane and dangerous sentiment which should be eradicated from planet earth. Dehumanizing Jewish peoples as devilish, sinister, or greedy manipulators diminish the entire human family; all peoples deserve dignity, justice, and love. All have something special to contribute to the good of the whole, including Jewish people. It must be understood, however, that opposition to the initial policies that established the state of Israel, the current violence and injustice perpetuated by Israeli toward the Palestinian peoples, can and should be separated from fallacious and hateful anti-Semitic attitudes and theological perspectives. One can be both anti-Israel and pro-Jewish. All Jewish people do not live in the state of Israel, nor do all Israeli citizens support the government of Israel. Indeed, the Jewish people have a history of suffering, but the current state of Israel is not above protest and criticism as one of the strongest military and intelligence powers in the world. The most widely published Palestinian Christian and theologian, Dr. Mitri Raheb, identifies the origin of pro-Zionist and anti-

Palestinian sentiments in the western world. He has served as a Lutheran pastor based in Bethlehem for three decades and brings a unique theological perspective on the establishment and defense of the government of Israel. Raheb reminds his readers of how the history of the Holocaust completely changed westerners' attitudes toward the Jewish population. In his view, the genocide of the 1930s of the Jewish diasporas in Europe has created a mindset among Americans and Europeans, that the Jewish people are forever vulnerable and constantly exposed to danger. Raheb suggests that the history of the holocaust has blinded the minds and numbed the hearts of Western Christians toward Palestinian suffering. The view exists, according to Raheb, that of all the victims of history, the Jewish people are preeminent.

In the aftermath of World War II, the foreign policies in the Western world shifted. It became standard policy that the Jewish people and by extension the state of Israel must be protected at all costs. This approach to Middle Eastern politics completely ignores the post-1948 suffering of the Palestinian population which has been inflicted upon them by the West. The late father Michael Prior expounds upon the irrationality of the Christian Zionists in their unquestioned support of Israel in its oppression of the Palestinians. Prior observes that...*biblical scholars and theologians in virtually every other arena inform their discussions with a sensitivity to the victims of oppression* (Prior 1997: 30).

They have since clung to the history of the 1930s suffering of the Jews, while dismissing Palestinian pain, according to Raheb. *I've struggled as a Palestinian living under Israeli occupation, feeling every single day the weight of its systemic humiliation, segregation, and oppression* (Raheb, 2017: 10). Professor Raheb is amazed by the paradox of viewing the seventh largest military of the world as the most vulnerable nation state while viewing one of the poorest population groups (the Palestinians) as a major threat to its existence. Raheb also points out the fact that such views are held by a great proportion of Western theologians. The fact that the state of Israel has developed into a nuclear power and a major intelligence and security state has not changed many minds, according to Raheb.

> *The fact that Israel has [Israel] has become the seventh-largest military power in the world, with nuclear weapons...does not take hold of Western consciousness. The impression one sometimes senses hearing the news in the United States is that Palestine is threatening Israel. Defending the security of the State of Israel thus becomes the ultimate "sacred cow... (Ibid, 21)."*

The history of the Holocaust as horrific and dehumanizing as it was, does not mean that the Israeli government is weak, helpless, and vulnerable to destruction by the poorest population groups of the Middle East. The state of Israel will remain strong regardless of comparably miniature threats to its safety and whatever it may have to give up in the name of peace. The fear industry by which Palestinians are oppressed is fed by too many Western theologians, particularly in the United States. The idea is that whatever is a threat to the modern state of Israel, the United States has the divine responsibility to combat. In their view the Palestinians are not humans to love and empower but to fear and combat. God will withdraw his blessings from the U.S., if they do not help Israel with the Palestinian threat is the thinking of too many American evangelicals. Nadera Kevorkian adds that representing Palestinians as threats to an imaginary divine mandate is dehumanizing. While secular Israel may not necessarily subscribe to the Israelology of Western, Christians, the fear of Palestinians as "threats" is held up before the U.S. public by the state. The idea is that if Palestinians are emboldened by driving Israel into the sea, they will also be emboldened to attack America. Kevorkian calls it "security theology."

> *The record of joining the biblical and the national has worked to obscure Palestinian presence and dispossession. Constructing colonized Palestinians as feared "threats" supported by securitized and biblical claims and justifications, sustains the settler state and enhances and naturalizes its power...On the present international scene, the Israeli security theology is supported by the global hegemon, the United States (Kevorkian 2015: 25).*

Such Israelology makes invisible the daily suffering and dehumanization of Palestinians while hyper-exaggerating the violent militancy of the population. The theology of American evangelicals surrounding the eschatology of Israel is so deeply rooted in their consciousness that their imaginary fear of the Palestinians is all that matters.

4.2 The Israeli Government is Subject to the Scrutiny of International Laws

One fact that must be considered is that neither modern Israel, nor ancient Israel is nor was above criticism and rebuke. The Old Testament prophets consistently prophesied against the crimes and injustices committed by ancient Israel, yet they were not considered anti-Semitic. Abuse of the poor, taking advantage of the widow and the fatherless, exploiting the foreigner, violence against the innocent, idolatry and injustices committed by Israel were condemned. These rebukes by the prophets were not designed to express hatred toward Israel, but to proclaim the lofty expectations of Israel's God. The fulfillment of such expectations was critical to receiving God's permission to remain in their land. Ancient Israel's settlement in Palestine was never guaranteed by virtue of their ethnic identity but by their willingness to show mercy and compassion to the most vulnerable members of their society. The Hebrew prophet Jeremiah proclaimed that if the prerequisites of justice and compassion were met, "*...then I will let you live in this place, in the land I gave your ancestors for ever and ever (Jeremiah 7:7." NIV.*) However, too often, Christian Zionist theologians assume that today's secular state of Israel, has unqualified and unlimited rights to settle Palestine and displace its longtime residence. Such theologians maintain such views, the state although today's Israel is not a religious theocracy, has little resemblance to the structure of ancient Israel, and commits crimes against humanity which violates the demands of the Old Testament and international law.

> *The promise of land always comes with covenant expectations for religious life and for justice, themes echoed regularly by the prophets...Modern Israel has made*

choices regarding the Palestinians living within its borders that would inspire harsh criticism from Old Testament prophets such as Amos or Isaiah (Younan, 2007).

Jesus also prophesied against Israel's hypocrisy. He called them snakes and a breed of vipers. He charged them with shutting out the marginalized and killing the prophets of old (Matthew 23:13-36). In his prophetic monologue of Matthew 23, Christ condemned Israel's love for religion, while neglecting God's highest priorities of *justice, mercy, and faithfulness.* There is no greater example of this than the Israeli occupation. While Jesus unabashedly and harshly rebuked Israel in his day, prominent American and Western theologians and clergy stubbornly refuse any constructive criticism of the state of Israel. Hagee asked, *why are we so tough toward our only friend in the Middle East, while apologizing for America's strength before nations sworn to our destruction* (Hagee 2010: 19)? What many Christian Zionist hardliners fail to recognize is that few U.S presidents or politicians are actually "tough" on Israel and rarely critique them due to fear of backlash from the political and religious right. What Hagee describes as tough, is simply requesting as diplomatically as possible that Israel comply with the international laws to which they have agreed. Zero tolerance toward the slightest criticism is what Hagee and others are demanding under the guise of not being tough on Israel. Ancient Israel faced formidable enemies from the time of David to Christ, yet the prophets and the Christ were tough on them for their injustices. Hagee argues that the Palestinians and their supporters are both America's and Israel's enemy. It is suggested that America and Israel are fighting the same battle. This leads the Zionist community in America to conclude that criticism of Israel is tantamount to disloyalty amid a holy war between the West and what they view as the Muslim world. They argue that such criticism of Israel is a show of weakness to their mutual Palestinian enemies and groups that stand up for their rights. Such ideas are not only theological, but are also born of cultural preservation, nationalism, racism, and militarism. Criticism of Israel and standing up for human rights is akin to treason against their tribe in their view. If they are equating the modern state of Israel with first century Israel, then Jesus himself must also be considered anti-Jewish, disloyal, and not respecting Western survivalism. This obviously is not the case. Christology upholds the view that Christ is the Word of God which takes preeminence over statecraft and nationalistic dreams and ambitions.

The Jewish holocaust was one of the most monstrous and diabolical injustices committed by a nation against an ethnic group. The Jewish diaspora in Europe suffered great persecution which climaxed with hateful Nazi regime of Germany in the 1930s. This history should serve as a reminder of the evils of xenophobia and where such attitudes may lead. Those Europeans who took dangerous risks and sacrificed their lives in support and defense of the Jewish people during the Holocaust are heroes on the right side of history.

The Jewish people deserve to live in freedom from xenophobia, violence, and persecution as members of the human family. When considering the need for Jewish land post World War II, an American colloquialism comes to mind: "Two wrongs don't make a right." While the Holocaust was wrong, so was Palestinian displacement and ethnic cleansing. The Palestinians were not responsible for the Holocaust, and it is unjust to lay the weight of historical European xenophobia on their backs.

The Palestinian people should never have had to suffer as a result of a European cultural and political wrongs. A better solution might have been for Europeans to provide land within its own continent and bear responsibility for its own hateful history toward the Jewish people. The dream of establishing a reborn biblical state of Israel was impractical, unnecessary, and never envisioned in the scriptures. Throughout history nations have risen and fallen, and populations have migrated from lands of origin. If every people group on earth were to trace the land of their ancestry thousands of years ago, go back to those places of their origin, drive out the current population, and establish their own nation, the world would never know peace. This is not an argument to end the state of Israel, but to critically examine the injustice toward Palestinians rooted in the history of post-World War II, so that such actions will be agreed upon as inhumane.

4.3 Acknowledgement of the Injustices Behind Israel's 1948 Establishment is Needed

Can one imagine if any or all population groups made efforts to leave their generational settlements to occupy populated land areas because their ancestors once lived there? Can anyone imagine the chaotic state of the world if such actions were to occur? Eric Fromm, a widely known scholar made a point of this in his publication in 1959. It must also be noted that the Jewish population of Europe had no connection to Palestine for nearly two-thousand years, while Palestinians remained there for the same period. There was no justice or justification in the Zionist vision for the initial establishment of Israel and the displacement and occupation of the Palestinians. Theologian Naim Ateek brings to light other entities which share the guilt in addition to Zionist Jews in their oppressive actions against the Palestinian people.

> *The guilt, however, cannot be borne by the Zionist Jews alone. It was due also to the political responsibility of Britain and the United States, as well as the biblical theology that many Western Christians espoused (Ateek 2017: 38).*

Since it is unlikely that the European nations and the United Nations cannot undo or reverse the decisions of the past, they should admit their horrible mistakes. This is urgently needed in order to pave the way for resolution in the Middle East conflict. There can be no resolution without the acknowledgement of wrongs committed.

The dream of peace in the Middle East is difficult to realize due to an unfortunate Eurocentric theology of Christian Zionism. This theology is quite prominent within the most powerful nation on earth. The Christian right in the US and the Israeli hardliners are close political partners on the world stage.

The Christian Right in the US are a major constituency within the Republican Party, which is one of the two major political parties. Zionism is commonly preached in American pulpits to Christian voters. It is taught that to criticize Israel, is to go against

God himself. Additionally, it is taught that Palestinians are irredeemably violent and enemies of God. The philosophy of this Zionist theology is carried into the US congress by their representatives and has even been welcomed by American presidents. These views are so strongly held, that when the U.S. president Jimmy Carter championed human rights in the Middle East, he was forthrightly condemned by fellow Christians. They stubbornly supported Israeli domination above all; not even the cry for human rights would stand in their way, according to professor Prior.

> *When President Carter [a devout Christian himself] shocked American Christian evangelical fundamentalists and charismatics with his concern for human rights and used the words 'Palestinian homeland' in a speech in March 1977, full-page advertisements, signed by prominent evangelicals, appeared throughout the USA [criticizing the speech] (Prior 1997: 26).*

The American president, Jimmy Carter, who was a devout Christian while in office, did not call for the extinction of Israel. He simply recognized the Palestinian homeland; history does not dispute nor deny this reality. It was his recognition that Palestinians had always lived there, and that human rights were being denied, that brought upon himself the anger of Christian Zionists. The Christian Zionist community is not unaware of the fact that Palestinians have always been there; they simply do not allow it to be spoken.

The mainstream political thinkers, such as those within the U.S. Democratic party, acquiesce to these right-wing ideas so as not to be charged with anti-Semitism and weakness against so-called American adversaries.

4.4 Zionist Theology is Erroneous, Contrary to Christian theology and Dehumanizing

What spirit lies behind the inhumane ideas of Zionist theology? Could it be that the political and cultural philosophy is the foundation for the theology rather than scripture? What are some of the beliefs of Christian Zionist theologians and those who are students of their teachings? In what ways are the bible used to justify the occupation and displacement of Palestinians? Primarily, Zionist theologians subscribe to the view that the establishment of the state of Israel was a fulfillment of prophecy. They subscribe to a theology that suggests that not only does the state of Israel have a divine mandate to occupy all of Palestine, but also that Christians have been divinely assigned to unequivocally support them.

> *They believe they have a biblical mandate to support the Jews as they return to and rule their ancient homeland. Some historical prominent leaders of this movement have been Hal Lindsey, the late Jerry Falwell, Pat Robertson, John Hagee, Tim LaHaye, John MacArthur, and Benny Hinn...theologians, ministries, and organizations (Nasserdan 2019: 2).*

The most prominent and influential white evangelical pro-Israel supporters in the United States have included Reverends Billy Graham, Franklin Graham, Pat Robertson and John Hagee and Dr. James Dobson. Hagee often argues that America and Europe are obligated to support the Israeli government militarily and financially in every endeavor to steal land from Palestinian families. Their theology demands both unwavering support and absolute sovereignty for Israel, despite human rights abuses. Additionally, Christian Zionists speak out against political leaders who criticize Israel's violation of international law, in its attempts to annex the entirety of Jerusalem and undermine human rights. In other words, Israel should only be supported, and never interfered with in its efforts to expand its borders. Notice the strong, harsh, and uncompromising language of Reverend John Hagee.

> *This land was given to Israel by covenant from God Almighty to Abraham 3,500 years ago and that covenant stands today! The president of the United States does not have the authority to tell the Jewish people they cannot live in East Jerusalem, their own capital, and/or in Judea and Samaria, where Jews have lived for millennia (Hagee 2010: 20).*

It must be noted that when Hagee mentions East Jerusalem, Judea, and Samaria, he is referring the West Bank, the Gaza Strip, and lands such as the Golan Heights. Additionally, he states that Jews have lived there for millennia, while ignoring the Palestinian presence for Millennia. Hagee glosses over the fact that the Jewish population had not recently lived there for over a thousand years. According to Hagee, Palestinians may be completely displaced from all their homes in favor of Israel's expansion because he believes theologically that God has given it to them. He is not satisfied with Israel merely living in safety within its current borders. It does not occur to such theologians, that the God of justice would never leave anyone homeless and in despair. The argument by Christian Zionists, such as Hagee, goes beyond the call for a Jewish state, but to finish a particular mission which includes displacing Palestinians from all their remaining lands. Praying for the peace of Jerusalem, a common theme in white Christian evangelical circles. This prayer, if indeed it is genuine and compassionate, should include the Palestinians of East Jerusalem. They too are inhabitants of that historic land. To exclude them in such a prayer would mean that only half of Jerusalem deserves to live in peace which is counterintuitive to such a prayer. While those Evangelicals who are hardliners for the occupation have the loudest voices, some have observed a theological shift on the horizon. They too must be mentioned as the American church's role in Palestinian suffering is explored.

> *A movement is building among justice-minded evangelicals. To them, the suffering of Palestinian civilians, including many siblings in Christ and those from diverse theological and faith traditions, demands accountability regarding the Israeli occupation…And this movement has gathered traction in recent years among young evangelical Christians who say figures like Hagee and Jeffress do not speak for them (Vaughn 2018: Sojourner article).*

Another organization called *Evangelicals for Social Action* have long been known to be openly sensitive to the pain of Palestinian living. This is a racially diverse group. Recently they have dropped the name "Evangelical" due to its antagonism to social justice and

Palestinian statehood. Another reason they dropped the name, was due to its association with ex-president Donald Trump who many believe is an encourager of Xenophobia. They now call themselves *Christians for Social Action.* While many in the group call themselves Evangelicals on an individual bases. This group advocates for human rights for Palestinians and rejects hardline and unequivocal support for Israel. It is unfortunate that their voices are not heard as loudly as hardline Christian Zionists (Cannon and Fisk 2021: Christians for Social Action Article).

What is the basis for the theology of Christian Zionism? It is the idea that the Jewish diaspora has been given a divine mandate to settle in the area of Palestine are based on promises made to the Israelite nation of scripture. What is often overlooked is that the promises of Israel reoccupying their Palestinian homeland were to be fulfilled after the time of the exile in Babylon. Another failure of Christian Zionism is in connecting a modern-day secular nation state operating under international law to the divinely established monarchy of ancient Israel. Additionally, Christian Zionists are so zealous in their support of Israel that they lose sight of Jesus' gospel of love, peace and healing. Jesus' message of love must have the pre-eminence in Christian theology. Christian Zionism is inconsistent with the work of and words of Jesus. When considering the harshness of the state of Israel toward the Palestinian population, along with unquestioned support of Israel, it is natural to question the basis for such a theology.

> *Christian Zionism takes the land promises of God in Genesis 12, 15, and 17 and applies them to the modern state of Israel...Therefore, despite Israel's own declared intention of being a secular state, modern Israel still benefits from a 4,000-year-old promise...the Abrahamic covenant is still active regardless of whether Israelis believe in God or not (Younan, 2007).*

Such theology is crafted by those who choose to view the scripture through Western lenses, rather than a Christological lens. Thus, this misguided theology is used to support Western interests above Christological interests in their efforts at world domination.

Genesis 12, 15 and 17 were fulfilled in the time of ancient Israel's settlement in Canaan, the expansion of its borders during the Davidic dynasty, and ultimately in Christ who shall eschatologically occupy the throne of David. It ignores that design of the Genesis prophecies. They provided land for a new nation who would represent the God who would eventually be born among them to save the world. The occupation of land by the Israelites was not the ultimate object but rather the means to ultimately fulfill that object. The object was to display the love and justice of God through Christ. These prophecies are mistaken to be permanent and unconditional and having application in the 20th and 21st centuries. Such views have been incredibly destructive to world peace by those who claim to serve the Prince of Peace. Moreover, it must be acknowledged that such views are not limited to European and American Christians, even though they are the loudest and politically strongest. Israel's political power is legally derived by international agreements, and its existence as a member of the international community is based on international law. Israel's legal rights are not based on claims of divine rights, which is a claim supported by Christian theology. Palestinian theologian and church leader, Naim Ateek addresses the issue as he sees it in the following words:

> *Israel considers itself an heir to the land by virtue of history—religious Jews would say by virtue of divine right. International law [which the government of Israel has agreed to follow as the standard for human rights in the world], however, states that the acquisition of territory by force is illegal and that Israel's occupation must end. Tragically, millions of Western Christians, as well as many Christians in Africa and Asia, accept Israel's claim because of their (mis) interpretation of the Bible (Ateek 2008: 50).*

Paramount in discussing the theology of Christian Zionism, is in understanding that its development is recent. This is not to suggest that dreams of Jews resettling in Israel had never been imagined. However, the modern-day theological views of Zionist theologians, its popularity among Christians, and the respectability occurred after the advocacy and rise of secular Zionism. Western nations have long had interest of having a presence in the Middle East for strategic and economic reasons, and secular Zionism became attractive in the U.S. and the West in that regard. Christianity in the west has had a history of competing for control of Palestine and the Middle East. The Crusades were a prime example of this. Considering this history, it became instinctive for Western theologians to incorporate ideas of establishing its influence in the Middle East through the resettlement of European Jews. If the Zionist Israelology is legitimate, why did it wait for the development of secular Zionism and the aftermath of War II and the empowerment of secular Zionism? European Jews are not the only branch of the diaspora. There is also Beta Israel of Ethiopia. Why was there no interest in resettling Beta Israel by the Western world, so much effort to settle European Jews? Why was there never a large-scale movement to settle Moroccan and Tunisian Jews in Palestine and establish a State? These questions must be answered in order to eliminate the stain of racism from Eurocentric theological Zionism. To suggest that that reestablishing Israel as a divine mandate needed to wait for the European Jewish Holocaust appears dishonest. Why was there so little movement on behalf of Beta Israel, by the state of Israel until long after its statecraft had been developed by those of European ancestry? Why do Ethiopian Jews struggle to assimilate within a Jewish state firmly rooted in their shared European background? *In the Israel of the 1980s and 90s, to which the Beta Israel emigrated, the standard rhetoric is that Israel must not repeat the 'mistakes of the 1950s', where large waves of Afro-Asian Jewish immigrants were treated as 'primitives...* (Schwarz 2017: 20).' If indeed Christian Zionism had legitimate concerns for a biblical mandate to resettle the Jewish population into Palestine, their advocacy for Beta-Israel of Ethiopia would have been on an equal basis with that of European Jewry.

4.5 The Secular Origins of Theological Zionism

Christian Zionism originated with efforts to advocate for secular Zionism through theological means. The father of modern-day Zionism, Theodor Herzl, had little interest in European Jewry resettling Palestine from a theological basis; it was strictly political and socio-economic. According to Ateek, Palestine was not Herzl's only vision for the establishment of a Jewish state. Argentina, the Sinai desert, Uganda, Cyprus was also considered as geographical areas for resettlement. His dreams of European Jews occupying Palestine developed later in his campaign for a Jewish homeland.

> *A Jewish state in Palestine was a stirring proposition, and not only for Jews. It could play on the emotions and garner the support of many western Christians, who saw in the Jews' return to Palestine a sign of the approaching eschaton, the coming again of Chris and the fulfillment of God's scheme for the future (Ateek 2014: 18).*

Herzl eventually settled on the idea of European Jews settling in Palestine as way to attract the support of Western Christians who view Jewish history from the perspective of the bible. Western Christians see a historical connection with the Jewish heroes of scripture such as Moses, Joshua, Solomon and King David. Herzl saw this as an opportunity to enlist the wealthiest and most influential population groups in his efforts to establish a Jewish state. This religious connection with Jewish history, he concluded would present Zionism as a divine movement in the earth. Settlement within Palestine by the European Jews would gain popularity within theological circles, more so than settling within Argentina or Uganda. This would also merge the interests of politicians and theologians for America and the West to have a foothold in the Middle East.

> *With the Bible as their sole guide, and observing the dispersion of the Jews, many Protestants applied certain exilic and post-exilic prophetic statements to their own times, thereby uncritically accepting the necessity of the return of the Jews to Palestine (Justice Ateek 2014: 19).*

Christian theologians misapplied prophetic statements by ancient prophets in support of the state of Israel and did so with little debate. Over time, these views became more solidified within American and European Christianity.

After the establishment of the state of Israel, theologians began to compare events happening in Palestine to Old Testament references and prophetic symbolism. The sensational nature of unfolding events in Palestine after 1948 garnered great interest and enthusiasm by those who viewed those militant activities as having eschatological implications. Eschatology is quite appealing because of the supernatural predictive nature it possesses. The idea that God is in full support of Israel and the Palestinians are acting against God's will took hold. The Palestinians began to be viewed as the enemies of God, Israel, and its supporters. This was the lens through which many Christians viewed the 1967 Israeli military campaign. The 1967 conquest of Palestinian territories, and the subsequent occupation and displacement of Palestinian families, instead of bringing tears to the eyes of Christians, was ironically met with cheers and celebration.

> *Israel's military victory in 1967 also had a huge impact on Christians worldwide. The David-and-Goliath myth circulated endlessly among many Christian groups globally, not only in the West. That victory was seen by many as divine intervention (Raheb 2014: 23).*

Today these views have become so entrenched that they are unchallenged and unquestioned. Alternative views are not welcomed within Christian theological circles. Although Christian theology calls for believers to speak out on behalf of the poor, oppressed and voiceless, any voice advocation for justice for Palestinians is viewed with disdain. Professor Michael Prior explains the roots of such views and how they are rooted in Colonialism.

> *Political Zionism, a child of the nineteenth-century European colonial age, has seduced the mainstream of Western thought also along those lines...Zionist ideology, detested from the beginning by virtually all shades of religious Jews, has been embraced by the establishment of virtually all sectors of Jewish religious opinion (Prior*

1999: 13).

Theologian Michael Prior, states that a moral analysis and critique of Israel's occupation of Palestine is unwelcomed by the Christian theological community. This is because this cuts at the grain of Western Christian identity which is linked unbreakably to Zionism. Prior refers to the pervasive nature of such theology both in conservative and mainstream Christian circles.

> *The view that the Bible provides the title deed for the establishment of the modern state of Israel and for its policies since 1948 is so pervasive, not only in both Christian Zionist and Jewish Zionist circles but even within mainstream Christian theology and university biblical studies, that the very attempt to discuss the issue is sure to encounter opposition (Prior 1997: 31).*

Christian theologians seem fearful that they will be viewed as rejecting Western values and as anti-Semitic. Such theological restraints allow for the subjugation of an entire population group that are made in the image of God. Advocacy by Christians for Palestinians is considered pro-Muslim and Anti-Christian, when in fact Christian Zionism is unchristian theologically and practically.

It must be clearly stated that Christian Israelology (as it is commonly constituted) is wrong both theologically and morally. "Isn't it simply helping to fulfill a biblical mandate?" some may ask. It is in fact in total opposition to the highest biblical mandate of love and care for the most vulnerable in the world. It diminishes and persecutes the humanity of the Palestinians which God created, and Christ redeemed. It advances empire building and militarism, which always becomes oppressive to the weaker members of the world. Christ declared that the last would be first and the first would be last. It violates Isaiah's mandate to *let the oppressed go free and to break every yoke* (Isaiah 58:6).

> *Palestinians are seen as having no rights to the land given by God to the Jewish people. In consequence, there is tremendous financial support from Western Christians for the Jewish people and the State of Israel and virtually no*

such support for Palestinians living in the "Holy Land" that belongs to the Jewish people (Munayer and Loden 2012: 45).

4.6 Christian Zionism's Militarism is Counterproductive to the Gospel of Peace and Love

When Christian Zionism is put into practice, it consistently places war over peace. Jesus called upon his followers to be peacemakers. The Christian right in America uses Old Testament language and promises to tie support of Israel to its own national prosperity. This is extremely ironic. Jesus said blessed are the peacemakers, not the warmongers. The militaristic language of Christian Zionists is counterproductive to the advancement of Christ's kingdom on Earth. Hagee argued that advocating for peace and making concessions in the Middle East is provocative, because it makes great powers appear weak, and invites violence by the Palestinians and their friends. He sees that the flexing of military power in the Middle East is essential to the preservation of Israel and America. *I think we need to understand it is never American strength that's provocative. What's provocative is America's weakness, and we are being very provocative today* (Hagee 2010: 31). Never does Christ suggest that working for peace results in violence against the peacemaker. This contradicts Christ's promise of blessing to the peacemakers of the Earth, and those who operate from a position of meekness. This view suggests that the threat of violence by the great powers in the Middle East is the solution that brings ultimate peace.

Christ never ordered his followers to use military power and intimidation to control and threaten a population as a means of accomplishing divine objectives as Hagee suggests. Christian theologians and clergy should be foremost in advocating for justice rather than advocating for the threat of war. Naim Ateek says, *instead of deterring injustice, they have exacerbated it by encouraging Israel's militancy* (Ateek 2014: 9).

The words of Christ and his lived experience on Earth, was in reality a representation of God's heavenly kingdom on earth. The life of Christ declares that the kingdom of God is about healing not wounding, mending broken hearts rather than further breaking them. It is about setting men free to live out their self-determined potential rather than imprisoning a population in hopelessness. This kingdom that Christ establishes seeks to open blinded eyes to a hopeful future, rather that blinding them with despair and dejection. Loosening the tongues of the dumb by Christ was an expression of the nature of God's kingdom on Earth. Yet, concerning the occupation by Israel, Mitri Raheb suggested, the *native peoples of the land (the Palestinians) were silenced politically by the military and economic occupation of their land and became theologically invisible* (Raheb 2014: 23). The Palestinians having no voice, and not allowed to protest oppression is counter to the principles of God's Kingdom. This kingdom, Christian theologians should strive to advance, rather than giving unequivocal support for a militant state of Israel.

While it may seem to the casual observer that there are no theological voices within White American Evangelicalism advocating for the human rights of Palestinians, but they do exist. Reverend Joel C. Hunter is among them. He fearlessly criticizes Israel as a friend, but advocates for a Palestinian human rights and statehood. He also disagrees with the right-wing preacher John Hagee's extremist positions in his unwavering uncritical support of the state of Israel. In his article in The Palestinian Chronicles reveals Hagee's extreme positions which include the idea that *the Palestinian people have never owned the land of Israel, never existed as an autonomous society.* Hunter states that while Hagee and others have the loudest voices, he believes they do not represent the majority of White Anglo-Saxon protestants.

> *There is a part of the evangelical family, which is what I call Christian Zionists, who are just so staunchly pro-Israel that Israel and their side can do no wrong, and it's almost anti-Biblical to criticize Israel for anything…But there are many more evangelicals who are really open and seek justice for both parties. (The Palestinian Chronicles, 2007)*

Reverend Hunter references theologian and historian Timothy Weber in his conclusion that Hagee and other dispensationalists are holding a minority view. It is his hope that the others can redeem what he believes is a false picture of evangelicalism painted by Hagee and his dispensationalist views. He cites Webber as stating the following:

> *'The dispensationalists (who interpret the Bible as predicting that in order for Christ to return, the Jews must gather in Israel, a third temple must be built and the Battle of Armageddon must be fought) have parlayed what is a distinctly minority position theologically within evangelicalism into a major political voice (Ibid. 2007).'*

It is commendable to see strong-minded Evangelical leaders standing up for the Palestinians as Jesus would have them. However, while Hunter and Weber are arguing that Hagee's position is only advocated by a minority, his views and those who think like him such as Franklin Graham are the only ones that are impacting U.S. policy in the Middle East. It is debatable that it is indeed a minority view. The US has not become less hardline politically when it comes to the state of Israel but is becoming more closely aligned with the rightist in Israeli politics as a result of their influence. Hunter and Weber's views, while making noble attempts, have little if any bearing on U.S. policy.

Christian theologians have utilized the Old Testament conquest narratives as a basis for Israel's persecution and displacement of the Palestinians through military means. Christian Zionism did not foresee the violence inflicted upon the Palestinians that would result in the establishment of Israel. They eventually began to accept and encourage it. Evangelical theologian, Les Nasserden presented a challenge to the Christian Zionists concerning its militarism, nationalism and ethnic partiality which so unlike the Christ of scripture.

> *Where, pray tell, does it say in the New Testament that Christians should give political and military support to the people/state of Israel? Christian Zionists also err when their efforts to minister to the legitimate practical needs of the people of Israel are not matched by similar efforts to minister to the legitimate practical needs of adjacent non-*

Jewish peoples (Nasserdan 2019: 58).

Christ never sided with the powerful against the weak and powerless, but drew near to the broken, oppressed ones, and those held captive. Christian theology should never favor one ethnic group as superior over another. New Testament theology declares that "God has made of one blood all peoples of the Earth (Acts 17:26)." This means that the Palestinians and Israelis are of the same blood and should be treated with the same respect. Dismissing the suffering of the Palestinians and advocating only for the prosperity of the state of Israel is inconsistent with the New Testament concept that says, "God is not a respecter of persons." Advocating for the overwhelming military force of the state of Israel, while criticizing the retaliatory violence of the Palestinians is hypocrisy.

One central theme throughout Christ's teaching was that of "setting captives free." Supporting the occupation of Palestinian territories is inconsistent with that theme of making humanity free. All populations have the right to be free to live out their God given existence, without interference as image bearers of the Divine. All populations, including the Palestinians, have a right to be free from ethnic cleansing, persecution, disenfranchisement, indefinite imprisonment, exploitation and humiliation. This disenfranchisement, which is supported indiscriminately by Christian theologians, is frighteningly similar to the policies of the white supremacist South African apartheid regime.

4.7 Christian Zionism reflects a Materialistic Spirit which Christ Condemned

It is disingenuous toward the Israelis and is extremely self-serving and materialistic. Is Zionist Israelology truly based on love for Israel or love for material wealth and prosperity? In many ways it appears that Western Christianity stands for the support of Israel not based on an ethical perspective but in the interests of its own prosperity.

Christian Zionists who advocate for the support of Israel in order to receive the promised Old Testament blessings come across as selfish and materialistic. Support of Israel is given in order to secure material blessings. New Testament theology advocates against materialism. It admonishes believers to *Love not the world, neither the things that are in the world, if any many loves the world, the love of the father is not in him...And the world passeth away, and the lust thereof, but he that doeth the will of the God abideth forever (1 John 2:15-1.7).* New Testament theology values humanity above material possessions and the systems of this world order. Christians are not to love material possessions but are commanded to love their neighbors as themselves. Zionism places national wealth, economic well-being, and security above the interests of the poor and the marginalized. These are the ones Christ most identified with. If it is true that support of Israel secures the financial prosperity of a nation, this would mean that world poverty would be eliminated simply by nation-states advocating for the security of Israel and the subjugation of the Palestinians. This is not what Zionist theologians are suggesting. They appear to suggest that these blessings singularly apply to America and the West. The blessings that are mentioned in the Gospels suggest that such material blessings are not promised to the proud, arrogant and militaristic peoples of the Earth. Christ's sermon on the Mount of Olives applies blessings not to the powerful or the great empires and dynasties who trample upon the rights of others, but to the meek, the poor in Spirit, the peacemakers, the persecuted, the merciful and the pure in heart (Matthew 5:1-11). One cannot be both militaristic and merciful as Christ defined it. One cannot ignore the pain of an entire population in order to obtain financial blessings from God. This is not considered *pure in heart*. One cannot be a meek nor a peacemaker by threats and intimidation. One cannot be persecuted by being a persecutor. Christ did not bring heaven to earth to grant material prosperity to empires, but to redeem suffering humanity. Yet Christian Zionism has fallen into the trap of serving mammon (material possessions) over God. Christ said one cannot serve both. The New Living Translation is worded in a way that explains the problems of materialism. It says, *"You cannot serve God and be enslaved to money (Matt. 6:24.)* Although Christ is clear in this matter, Zionism elevates materialism above human compassion. Notice the language of one American Zionist who conditions the material prosperity and the technological advancement of his country upon being a blessing and a friend of the state of Israel. It reveals that self-interested nature of Christian Zionism, whereas Christ taught that it is more blessed to give than to receive.

> *"God has blessed America because America has blessed the Jew," said Jerry Falwell, invoking this verse in 1980. "If this nation wants her fields to remain white with grain, her scientific achievements to remain notable, and her freedom to remain intact, America must continue to stand with Israel" (Spector 2008: 24).*

What is overlooked and ignored by Christian Zionists such as Falwell, is that American freedom (according to their theology) is dependent on the bondage of Palestinians. Their economic advancement is dependent upon the unemployment and impoverishment of the Palestinians. Their scientific achievements must be built on the backs of the illiteracy and miseducation of the Palestinians. The Kingdom of Christ would never deny the freedom to one group by denying the freedom of another. Enriching the powerful by depriving those in poverty is the antithesis of what the Kingdom of Christ came to accomplish. The coming of the Messiah is described in Luke as pulling down the mighty from their seats and exalting the lowly. It is about *filling the hunger with good things and sending the rich away empty* (Luke 1:15). Yet, Christian Zionism advances the exact opposite of God's ideal in Christ. Such blessings, according to Zionist theology would be the fruits and benefits of exploitation, displacement, imprisonment and oppression.

The irony of Christians who support unequivocally Israel's military action against a defenseless Palestinian Christian family and poor Muslims is profound. Christian Zionism contradicts the gospel of Jesus Christ of Nazareth completely and unapologetically. It fails to recognize the foundational basis for interpreting and advancing theological positions. The late theologian professor James Cone outlines what Christ represented as the revelation of God in the Earth, which involved uplifting the poor and countering injustice.

The hermeneutical principle for an exegesis of the Scriptures is the revelation of God in Christ as the Liberator of the oppressed from social oppression and to political struggle, wherein the poor recognize that their fight against poverty and injustice is not only consistent with the gospel but is the gospel of Jesus Christ (Cone 1997: 133).

Christian Zionism pits unwittingly pits the Western Christian militarily against the Palestinian Christian. Therefore, Christian Zionism fails to fulfill Christ's commands to Christians to love one another and lay down their lives for fellow disciples. Rather than laying down one's life for the fellow Christian, Christian Zionism allows for the displacement, the ethnic cleansing and the taking of the lives of fellow Christians. *Approximately 60 percent of the Christians were ethnically cleansed. The loss of Christian numbers weakened the church further* (Ateek 2017: 31). Some may argue that such actions would never occur against any other segment of the Christian world. According to Zionist theology, the security of Israel is more important that the survival of the Christians of Bethlehem or Nazareth. Instead of helping the Christian population advance its work of love, reconciliation and its service to humanity, Christian Zionism helps to destroy such a work

4.8 The Contemporary state of Israel is Not the Same Entity as the Israel of Antiquity

It is theologically incorrect to suggest that the modern state of Israel and ancient biblical Israel are the same. The modern state of Israel is a secular state which functions under international law rather than religious law. Both after the Exodus from Egypt and the Babylonian exile period, the nation of Israel was established by divine law. Each settlement back into Palestine was divinely directed. In the case of the modern state of Israel, resettlement was directed by European nations. Additionally, it focused singularly upon the Jewish population of Europe to the exclusion of those of North Africa and Ethiopia. In each of ancient Israel's return from captivity, their survival in the land of Palestine was conditional upon their obedience divinely given laws and commands. Ancient

Israel was only allowed to exist as a nation as long as they obeyed the divine mandate. However, the United Nations and the international community guarantees unconditionally the permanent settlement of Israel in Palestine. The Israeli government is only held accountable to uphold international laws and norms, yet its survival is not based on acquiescence to such laws. Christian Zionists seek to uphold by force the survival of Israel regardless of compliance with divine or international law.

> *The land promise of the divine covenant associated with Abraham, Moses, and the Old Testament prophets was and is conditional on faith and obedience. The reunification of the people and land of Israel in 1948 CE was humankind's arbitrary attempt, without faith and obedience…to undo what God sovereignly decreed two to four thousand years ago (Nasserdan 2019: 60).*

God did not divinely choose the modern state of Israel to be established in the Middle East; it was established through secular political bodies for the service of Western interests. The establishment of Israel provided an asylum from European xenophobia, but the European partners simultaneously benefited. The idea of "chosen people," drawn from Old Testament language and utilized for nationalistic and imperialistic aims should be theologically re-examined. This is the view of Father Ateek.

> *This testimony to the oppressive underside of the biblical motifs of God's liberation of one chosen people must call us all to question exclusivist concepts of peoplehood and God. It must call us back to the universalist direction of the three faiths, not as imperialist denial of particularity, but as the global context in which particularities of peoplehood, culture, and nationalism can be reconciled and we can learn to live as neighbors sharing one land, sharing one earth. (Ateek 2014: 6)*

If the modern secular state of Israel was indeed chosen, it was chosen by secular Zionists, the United States, Europe and the United Nations. The religious/political nation of ancient Israel ended during the time of the Roman Empire. There is no divine mandate to displace and oppress the Palestinians in the name of fulfilling an imaginary eschatological mandate. The state of Israel is governed by its own secular parliament and prime ministers and functions by its own secular laws. Bishop Munib Younan of the Evangelical Lutheran Church in Palestine dispute the common view that the modern-day nation existing under the name of Israel and ancient Israel are the same.

> *The assumption that the modern state of Israel today equates to Biblical Israel of ancient times is very problematic. The Jews come to this land because they were persecuted by European nations. The modern state of Israel is a full member of the international community of nations, having accepted the major tenets of international law and conventions (Younan, 2007).*

In ancient times, there were prophets that gave instructions on resettlement and re-establishment. They gave instructions on the divine laws that would govern them. There were no prophets that were raised up within Judaism post-World War II to give direction to the Jewish diaspora about the re-establishment of ancient Israel nor resettlement of Palestine. There was no "word from the Lord." The vision for a modern state of Israel did not come through divine revelation, but through collaboration among European and leading nations of the world in response to the aspirations of Zionists.

4.9 Theological Zionism Supports the Oppression which Christian Theology Condemns

Moreover, the occupation of Palestine and subsequent oppression of Palestinians is inconsistent and contrary to what Jesus fought against in that very land. The actions of Christian Zionism and Israeli occupation is more consistent with the Roman occupation of Jesus' day than the beliefs and ethics of early Christianity. Jesus both suffered and overcame such oppression. The suffering that the Palestinians have come to experience is similar to that which Jesus understood and experienced. It is ironic that the theology of Christian Zionism is aligned historically with the Roman occupiers of the first century than Jesus and those he lived among. Such theology and its influence on politics has a striking resemblance to the political philosophy of Roman Empire of Christ's day. It is amazing that the suffering of the Christian and Muslim Palestinians is the same suffering that Jesus sought to alleviate, yet the theology of Christian Zionists adds to their suffering. It is quite paradoxical that Muslims, who do not elevate Christ as do Christians, speak out against injustice and oppression in the Middle East. Their radical call for justice and peace is more Christlike than the sermons by Christian theologians who speak out so strongly in favor of Israel's occupation and security interests. What is overlooked by Zionist theology is that the Palestinians are an oppressed people and Jesus counted himself among the oppressed. The suffering and victimization of the Palestinians is the suffering and victimization of Jesus. This is the Christological perspective that is missing in Zionist theology.

4.10 Christian Zionism Violates the Designs of an Inclusive God who Identified with

Displaced and Landless People

Christian Zionism, when put into practice is extremely problematic. It diminishes and works against human flourishing. This places it in conflict with the gospel of Jesus Christ which advocates for healing, human progress and human advancement. This may not be the intention of such theologians, but the unintended side effects are the crippled and paralyzed existence of an entire population of creatures for whom God cares. Professor Mitri Raheb decries Western Christianity's limited focus concerning the cross of Calvary. A great proportion of Western Christianity, when reflecting upon the cross, focus almost solely on the forgiveness of sins and the way opened to heaven. He suggests that Christ also died because he sought to bring heaven to earth in his concern for God's creatures.

> *He came to bring heaven's values—God's care for all creatures—to earth." And what happened to him? He paid a steep price. He was heckled; he came under surveillance; he was arrested; he was tortured; and he was*

executed...because he cast a bold vision for human flourishing in the midst of human suffering (Raheb and Henderson 2017: 11).

Zionist theology oftentimes reflects self-centeredness and undermines the reality of a universal and inclusive God. It appears to Palestinians that it is a philosophy that supports the violence and displacement of a Palestinian community who lived on the land for thousands of years. As Palestinian Father Naim Ateek eloquently stated, *The Jewish claim to the promised land is their dispossession from their land of Palestine. Jewish peoplehood excludes the existence of Palestinians as a people. Jewish redemption is Palestinian oppression* (Ateek 2014: 7).

The prophet Ezekiel introduces an inclusive God, who has designed that land must be shared as a basic human need. According to Ezekiel, God does not allow for population removal, landlessness or homelessness when they return. Ezekiel's points the way to the period of Israel's return from exile and provides instruction on their treatment of those who they will meet when they arrive. His prophetic utterance gives no room for oppression nor second class citizenship for those who already dwell in the land. He says, *You shall altot it as an inheritance for yourselves and for the aliens who reside among you and have begotten children among you. They shall be to you as citizens of Israel (Ezekiel 47:21-22)."* Theological Zionism far too often fails to uphold this moral principle and shows no concern for Palestinian displacement. Those who advocate these views draw a connection between the military battles of the Old Testament in the time of Joshua when Israel entered Canaan. They fail to include in their theology the prophetic declarations of Jeremiah, which depicts the heart of God as identifying with the displaced and oppressed. Professors R. Kendall Soulen and Linda Woodhead provide helpful analysis through Jeremiah's writings concerning Israel's place in Palestine in contrast to the early Old Testament conquest history.

There is no conquest of Canaan in Jeremiah's account, so he does not depict the divinity as a mighty warrior driving

> *out enemies who have polluted the land and must be expelled prior to Israel's settlement (Lev. 18:2430) (Soulen and Woodhead 2006: 140).*

Although the Jeremiah is capturing the experience of ancient Israel, the devastation, and the terror of being a refugee who is displaced and insecure is evident. It expresses the horror of any human being or population group who has nowhere to go and cannot be at rest. These experiences are not limited to Israel. The experiences that are expressed in Jeremiah, although it is referencing ancient Israel, are strikingly like the horrors of the ongoing displacement of the Palestinian people. *The Palestinian refugees represent the largest and most protracted refugee problem in the world* (Samy 2010: 37). Ironically, the Palestinians may identify more closely with Jeremiah's description of the displaced than any other people group in the world. Jeremiah expresses the sadness of being uprooted and having nowhere to go because the sword is on every side (Jeremiah 6:25). There are Palestinian families who have been driven from one home to another over the decades of Israel's founding, due to their expansionist ambitions. The pain of those who suffer from displacement, landlessness and homelessness is God's own pain, according to Professor Linda Woodhead's interpretation of Jeremiah. To dismiss or overlook the pain of the suffering Palestinians is to be dismissive and unconcerned with God's own pain. This is the dilemma of Zionism in all its forms. It appears that it is almost impossible to view a displaced people as enemies and yet identify with the heart of God.

> *Among Jeremiah's many portraits of divine suffering over the separation of people and land, his fleeting depiction of YHWH as a homeless wanderer, seeking nothing more than a place to rest for the night (14:8), lingers in memory (Soulen and Woodhead 2006: 151).*

It is clear from Jeremiah's writings that divinity stands in solidarity with the displaced and enters their grief and suffering. According to Jeremiah, divinity is not identifying with those who wield the sword and bring about homelessness and despair. If divinity cannot rest due to the separation of people and land, neither should Christians, Muslims and Jews. When Christians seek to alleviate the pain of Palestinians in their occupation, they are understanding the heart of the divine and helping alleviate the pain of divinity. When Christians seek to alleviate the restlessness of the Palestinians, it should also ease their own restlessness which comes from feeling the pain of the displaced. The inability to feel such restlessness is the inability to feel the heart of the divine. Their cries are God's own cries. Having land upon which one may rest and be at peace is a part of God's ideal for human existence. Advocating for the displaced and for the liberation of the captive should be the work of the Christian in bringing the kingdom and will of God to Earth as it is in heaven. Christian Zionism completely fails in this regard. God sees the Palestinian crisis, the causes of their grief and the victims of Zionist theology. He sees the horrors of displacement, the indignities that his image-bearers suffer, and the dehumanizing experiences they bear daily.

The Palestinians do not have citizenship in most cases in the surrounding countries where they have found asylum. As refugees they become stateless non-citizens without the right to vote or self-determination. To grant them citizenship would be counterproductive to the Palestinian struggle for their own national identity and right to return. This has been an ongoing crisis for four generations. In the modern political order, the lack of citizenship rights is the equivalent to the denial of human rights.

> *The classical order of nation-state has thus developed rights for citizens but not for human beings. As Hannah Arendt noted as early as the beginning of the 1950s, there is no place for the human being outside the nation-state. There are citizens' rights but not human rights (Ibid., 38).*

The same Zionist principles that cause the displacement of the Palestinians has also created a refugee crisis throughout the Muslim world, due to wars brought to Muslim countries by the West. Militant groups in the Middle East are viewed as an existential threat to Israel, which in order to save Israel, must be fought. Dr. Stephen Spector is a Christian who is a professor at

Stony Brook University. He is ethnically Jewish but disagrees with the militant ideas of Evangelical Zionists. He sets forth the underlying reasons for the unlikely alliance of Evangelicals and hardline Zionists.

> *The Israeli-Palestinian dispute is one of the most hotly contested questions in the world, freighted with existential fears and elemental indignation and rage. Adding the conservative Christian marriage of faith and politics to that dangerous mix heightens the intensity of the debate. That is all the more true because many Christian Zionists consider themselves to be naturally allied with Jews against a radical Islamist movement. (Spector 2008: 4).*

Spector expanded upon what he viewed as a usual alliance when he referenced a conversation, he held with a young evangelical who said. *The danger is Islamic extremism. The world is changing...Europe is all but lost. Western values are at stake and Israel represents the frontline (ibid., 9).* (One of the mistakes that American Evangelicals make is to conflate Christian principles with Western values, when in fact Christianity began in the Middle East and North Africa.) The changes they see in the world is a cause for concern for them. This fear was one of the rationales for the 2003 American invasions of Iraq, and its recent military actions in Syria. Theological Zionism, while advocating Christocentric values, perhaps unwittingly, contributes to the stateless existence of Palestinian refugees, and their lack of human rights. Israel's militarism and aggression is supported, advocated for, and applauded by mainstream Christians in the West. Western nations seem to feel that it is their God-given right to invade Muslim lands in order to further its interests; they fail to respect, Palestinian, Arab, and Asian populations as equally human. Soulen and Woodhead approach this issue and appeals to Christian and theologians. There is little sympathy for the painful existence of Palestinian refugees by those theologians who advocate for militant Israeli politics.

> *The crisis challenges Christians everywhere to reflect theologically and practically about how our understanding*

of humanity as the image of God, who has been extended the promise of life abundant, might apply to masses of displaced persons existing in degraded and seemingly hopeless conditions (Soulen and Woodhead 2006: 135).

4.11 Theological Zionism Devalues Palestinian Humanity which Christ Redeemed

Zionist theology too often fails to uphold Palestinian humanity as equally valuable to the humanity of Israelis, Europeans, and Americans. The same desires and aspirations which European's desire and hope for their children and future generations are the same desires and hopes of the Palestinians. The same hunger for life and liberty that Westerns seek for themselves are the same hungers that all humanity seeks for themselves and their kindred. Europeans and Israelis would rather that Palestinians not protest or resist their occupation and displacement, would they not do the same if met with the same circumstances. Christ's work to set men free was evident in his earthly ministry. This work did not end when he died and ascended to glory. This means that wherever there is a struggle in the world to be free, it is God's own struggle. To blame the Palestinian's plight on their efforts to be free from subjugation and humiliation is an attitude of hostility toward the kingdom of God. It is the same hostility that caused the Roman occupiers to hang Jesus on the cross. Zionist theology is more akin the ambitions of the Roman occupiers of Palestine in the first century, than the Kingdom of peace that Christ represented in contrast. In order to achieve peace on Earth, Christian theologians must analyze the implications of Zionism and its awful impact on humanity. There is far too much dependence and faith in military power, among Christian Zionists in America than the principles of the Kingdom of God. There appears to be a fear that peacemaking, diplomacy, and love for humanity cannot triumph. The true exercise of faith will not rely so heavily on military power but will trust that compassion, dignity, and respect will bear the fruits of a better world.

What is more troubling and complicated about many of the ideas of theological Zionism are that it appears not be rooted in historic Christianity but colonialist and empire ideals of secular Zionism. Kristin Kobes Du Mez, professor of History at Calvin University, writes about the conflicted history of Evangelicalism, its connection with Israeli hardliners. Through the lens of history, she offers the key to getting back on the path of righteousness.

> *ACROSS TWO MILLENNIA of Christian history—and within the history of evangelicalism itself—there is ample precedent for sexism, racism, xenophobia, violence, and imperial designs. But there are also expressions of the Christian faith—and of evangelical Christianity—that have disrupted the status quo and challenged systems of privilege and power. (Du Mez 2020: 17)*

Evangelical leaders have an opportunity in this age to correct its course and embrace its legacy of freedom fighting rather than aligning itself with the most powerful in the world. The Palestinian/Israel conflict is one in which faith can triumph over fear and the love of Christ can be revealed.

The secular roots of Zionism cannot be denied. Many students of history mistakenly conclude that the idea for the establishment of the state of Israel began in the aftermath of the Jewish Holocaust. It is an incorrect belief that the policy for the establishment of the state of Israel in 1948 was born of a long held spiritual and religious vision. The theological views of Zionism developed after the dreams and visions of secular Zionism. It must be remembered that secular Zionism developed in a time when colonialism and racism was at its height. Settling into other countries, subjugating their populations and exploiting their resources were considered as a normal exercise of European privileges. Before there was ever any widespread theology of Zionism, secular Zionists laid plans for the oppression and removal of the Palestinians. Christian Zionism was sold to Western theologians by secular Zionists in order to help facilitate those ambitions. The means to fulfill those ends were unethical, immoral, sinister and dehumanizing toward the Palestinians. The most vocal political leader in the growth of both secular and eventually theological Zionism was Theodor Herzl. It is obvious through his own words that Herzl had little regard for Palestinian humanity.

> *[Herzl's population transfer plans included calls to] '...expel the poor population across the border unnoticed, procuring employment for it in the transit countries, but denying it any employment in our own country'. He added that both 'the process of expropriation and the removal of the poor must be carried out discreetly and circumspectly (Prior 1999: 22).'*

Herzl's ambitions were evident and should never have been supported by Christian theologians. The gospel of Jesus is always good news to the poor and never disregards the flourishing and elevation of the poor.

Another misleading conclusion that many have drawn concerning theological Zionism is that the Jewish diaspora in had long held the dream of migrating to the Middle East and establishing a new Israel. The reality is that the present iteration of Zionism is quite recent. Reformed Jews did not support the efforts of Zionists to form a nation in Palestine but condemned these efforts as late as 1919. It was roundly resisted within Rabbinical circles as inconsistent with the ethics of Judaism. Herzl's propositions were opposed by them. According to Father Michael Prior, Chief Rabbi Mortiz Gudemann of Vienna, was foremost among those who were in opposition to Herzl's ambitions. Rabbi Gudemann viewed these efforts as a violation of their religious beliefs and teachings.

> *Chief Rabbi Moritz Güdemann of Vienna, maintained that the Jews were not a nation, and that Zionism was incompatible with the teachings of Judaism...Rabbis representing all shades of opinion denounced Zionism as a fanaticism and contrary to the Jewish scriptures and affirmed their loyalty to Germany (Ibid., 1999: 18).*

The idea that Jewish clergy did not initially support the

establishment of the state of Israel is often overlooked. However, it needs to be a part of the diplomatic discussions in order to inform future efforts at justice and peace.

4.12 The Secular Zionism Embraced by Theologians Reflected Many Racist and Colonialist Ideas

Secular Zionism was based on the ideas of racial superiority which held dehumanizing views toward the occupants of the Middle East. There is spiritual link between the racialized ideas of conquest by historic Eurocentric Christianity and the embrace of Zionism by Christian theologians. The ideas of Christian colonialism held that Europeans were morally superior religiously and culturally to the inhabitants of Asia and Africa, and it was their duty to occupy their lands and civilize an inferior people. Colonialism viewed Africa and the Near East as barbaric, illiterate, and savage, and unworthy of being respect with the full dignity that human beings deserve; Zionism presented a new branch from the same racist and imperialistic tree. The Jewish people had assimilated over thousands of years in the lands and among the people which they settled. They were not limited to Europe but existed in Africa and Asia. Herzl focused on repatriating those with European heritage for a reason which is racial in its underpinning. Christian theology, if it is to be a force for good in the world should have nothing to do with it.

> *Herzl presented the proposed Jewish state as 'a portion of the rampart of Europe against Asia, an outpost of civilization opposed to barbarism' He reflects European racist superiority. Jews returning to their 'historic fatherland' would do so as representatives of Western civilization, bringing 'cleanliness, and order to this plague-ridden, blighted corner of the Orient (Ibid., 1999: 18).*

The truth of the matter is that the Middle East and Africa did not have an inferior culture but were all great people with values, morals and aspirations for the future. Neither Zionism nor colonialism brought cleanliness and order to those lands they invaded, but brought with them the filth of oppression, racism, displacement, violence, and cruelty. This is the true plague which continues to contaminate the world to this very day. They did not cure the world of any blight, but contaminated the lands they discovered with hatred, greed, and war. It is a stunning admission that the European Jews were chosen by Zionists for the settlement of Palestine because of their partial European ancestry. Zionism has its roots in racial superiority. This often comes into consideration when Palestinians are viewed as barbaric and violent, and Israel is seen as a shining light and a friend of the West. The foreign policy of Western nations sides heavily on the side of the state of Israel, while Palestinian leaders are condemned and assassinated. No European nation would have ever been subjected to the persecution and oppression which the Palestinians have experienced. When the world powers learn to respect the dignity of all humanity, the world will have hope of peace and tranquility.

4.13 Palestine Not the Only Option for Jewish Resettlement

Another erroneous assumption that is made by many political observers is that Palestine was the only option for Jewish resettlement. The establishment of the state of Israel in Palestine was not the initial action plan in response to Hitler's genocide. In fact, various countries stepped forward to welcome thousands of European Jews as refugees. According to Michael Prior, *Uganda was also considered as a place for resettlement (Ibid., 20).* European countries stepped forward along with the United States One of the issues that European democracies faced, is that their voters were oftentimes unwilling pay the cost of taking in Jewish immigrants. If Jewish asylum seekers could find another place that would not burden their countries' economies, they would encourage the policy. Prior also informs his readers that the U.S. president Roosevelt was resistant to Zionist aims, but when Roosevelt died, Zionism found new life. The new president of the U.S. was Harry Truman, a friend of the Zionist movement. Truman found that Jewish resettlement in Palestine was good politics because it would relieve America of the burden of taking on so many refugees.

Truman might have received, at America's expense, some

of the 300,000 survivors of the Nazi barbarism. His tactic gave him a double victory, winning the support of the Zionists, and allaying all fears that the USA might bear the brunt of Jewish immigration (Ibid., 34).

Secular and Christian Zionism accomplished two objectives that benefited Western nations. Firstly, it removed the expense and responsibility of Western nations following the Jewish Holocaust following World War II. Additionally, it provided an opportunity for the West to vicariously colonize Palestine for geopolitical interests. Tragically, the Palestinian population was forced to pay a horrific expense and a tremendous crippling burden, not of welcoming immigrants, but by being subjected to occupation, colonization, and oppression. It is inconceivable that the poorer nations should buckle under the weight of burdens which Westerners would never imagine having to bear. The choice was easy; the richer nations should have welcomed the Jewish immigrants, rather than shifting the responsibility to the Palestinians and forcing them to be displaced or live under undesirable conditions. The Palestinians were forced to suffer for the political expedience and convenience of the West. This political tactic is the very opposite of the justice and equity which Christian theology demands. When considering the historical roots of Christian Zionism, and the racialized politics that preceded it, we may conclude what has been known by oppressed groups from time immemorial. Mitri Rabeb's words capture the spirit behind theological Zionism when he said the following. *Empires create their own theologies to justify their occupation* (Raheb 2014: 12).

We must rightly conclude that if there is ever to be reconciliation between the oppressed and the oppressor, both political policies and theologies of racial superiority must end.

4.14 Redeemed Humanity (not Government or Empires) Has Rights to Exist

Whenever there is conflict in the Middle East between the Palestinians and the Israeli government, the common refrain that often spoken by Christian theologians and politicians is that Israel has the right to exist. These words are spoken while Palestinian neighborhoods are being bombed and innocent children are killed. Many argue that the Palestinians are seeking to drive the Israelis into the Mediterranean Sea. The words spoken by Palestinian fighters concerning driving Israel into the Sea is mere hyperbole uttered by an oppressed people. Such speech is common among the oppressed.

The Palestinian militias, with defective and primitive weaponry, do not have and will not have for generations to come the power to drive the Israel into the sea. This hyperbole spoken by Palestinian militants, as weak as they may be, have been utilized by Christian Zionists for their own purposes. The reality is that the Palestinians are being driven metaphorically into the sea through demolition of Palestinian homes, and the creation of illegal Jewish settlements in contemporary Palestinian areas.

> *Palestinian refugees presently stand as the largest and most protracted case of displacement in the world. The first massive wave of exodus, displacing about two-thirds of the entire Palestinian population, began in the late 1940s... about 60 per cent of Palestinian refugees are stateless persons with no recognized citizenship (Samy 2010: 23).*

Palestinians asserting their humanity through militant expression is used to justify cruel occupation, checkpoints, and overwhelming military force against its impoverished population. It is urged upon the citizens of Western nations, that the Palestinian people are a threat to Israel's existence, and therefore Israel's militarism is justified. Very few theological voices from the Western theological circles make unequivocal declarations that the Palestinians have the right to exist in dignity and in freedom. It is true that the Israelis need security, however the government has superior surveillance and other policing resources to apprehend rather than bomb and destroy. Respect for Palestinian dignity, diplomacy, sympathy, and compassion are the greatest tools in Israel's arsenal to resolve the crisis. Christian theology suggests that the strongest should be the first to help the weakest, and theologians should push Israel in that direction. Israel has the tremendous reserves to alleviate Palestinian suffering and maintain security.

No government, nation, empire, or kingdom has ever had the inherent right to exist. The Torah teaches that ancient Israel occupied land which belonged to God, which He allowed them to settle as foreign tenants on a temporary basis. Leviticus 25:23 says, *The land is not to be permanently sold because it is Mine, and you are only foreigners and temporary residents on My land* (Holman Christian Standard Version, 2009). No nation, whether it be China, Russia, Canada or Kenya, has the right to exist. Humanity has been granted by God the right to exist, and not governments or dynasties. Peoplehood is more important than statehood. There is no guarantee that any nation will survive, but the survival of humanity is non-negotiable from a theological anthropological perspective. Nations have risen and fallen throughout history, and in many cases for the good of humanity. They exist by the permission of a higher power to which they are accountable. This includes the state of Israel. It is also true that no nation has the right to trample the weak, subjugate the impoverished and destroy the lives which the creator has made. No nation has the right to steal property from other people in order to achieve its national designs. This should never occur, particularly with the support of theologians. It must be remembered that land borrowed from God by nations on the condition that they behave justly. The Torah clearly says, *follow justice and justice alone, so that **you** may live and possess **the land** the LORD your God is giving you (Due. 16:20 NIV)*. The state of Israel consistently violates international laws which it has agreed to uphold and has failed to exercise justice toward the Palestinian population. This injustice, which is largely supported by US evangelicals does not take in consideration how much land is being unjustly extracted by Israel and how much is being sacrificed by the Palestinians. Father Ateek compares the offers of peace by the Palestinians in-spite-of the continued injustices and bad faith actions by the Israeli government.

> *The Palestinian offer of peace to Israel is actually generous. Palestinians are willing to accept Israel as a state and to allow Israel to maintain 78 percent of the land instead of the 55 percent assigned to it by the United Nations. Yet Israel continues to shun and reject this offer.*

> *For the sake of peace most Palestinians are ready to absorb a further injustice so they can live in security on only 22 percent of the area of Palestine (Ateek 2008: 50).*

It is God's eschatological ideal that human beings be able sit *under their own vine and fig tree, where none should make them afraid.* This expression is rendered three times in the Old Testament in Micah 4:4, 1 Kings 4:25, and Zechariah 3:10. Israeli occupation violates this ideal. The Israeli government views Palestinian protest and resistance as a national security threat, and the population suffers in consequence. It is as if they wish they would die quietly without any protest or resistance. Many ask that we pray for the peace of Jerusalem based upon the popular Psalm, but peace is not merely the absence of conflict, but the presence of God manifested by the love displayed by his worshippers. This mindset within Eurocentric theology, which calls for the State of Israel to conquer the Palestinian territories, is a direct violation of the command of Jesus to love your neighbor as yourself. This means placing yourself in another person's shoes and questioning whether one would love to be treated the same under similar circumstances. Jesus taught, in the good Samaritan parable, that one's neighbor includes more than one's own countryperson. It includes anyone we meet along the road who needs compassion. The theology of peace, love, reconciliation and hospitality has been lost sight by many Christian theologians for a theology of conquest and subjugation around the topic of Israel/Palestinian relations. Leading theologian, Terrence Tilley authors a book entitled "The Disciples Jesus" which explores reconciling practices that are demanded of all who are disciples of Jesus. Tilley quotes Levine in his commentary upon the parable of the Good Samaritan and how it relates to today's world,

> *To understand the parable in theological terms, we need to be able to see the image of God in everyone, not just members of our group...The ancient kingdom of Samaria is, today, the West Bank. Thus, translated across the centuries, the parable retains the same meaning. The man in the ditch is an Israeli Jew; a rabbi and a Jewish member of the Israeli Knesset fail to help the wounded man, but a member*

of Hamas shows him compassion. If that scenario could be imagined by anyone in the Middle East, perhaps there might be more hope for peace. (Tilley 2008: 191)

There is little room for Palestinian dignity and humanity in the modern hardline Evangelical theology surrounding Israel. There is also little consideration, respect or love for the historical Palestinian Christians who are being oppressed along with their Muslim neighbors. These Palestinian Christians are among the oldest group of Christians in the world; it is the land where Christ's followers were established. It appears that there is little concern for their fellow Christians in that part of the world. Through the beliefs and policies of Western Christianity, suffering and pain has been inflicted upon fellow Christians. Through the influence of secular and Christian Zionists in the U.S., billions of dollars are given to the oppressive government of Israel. The $3 billion dollars which is granted annually by the United States through foreign aid to Israel, is being used to displace and humiliate Palestinian Christians who should be supported by their fellow believers. They should be joining hands with their fellow Palestinian Christians in spreading the love of Jesus and fulfilling his demand for justice for the oppressed throughout the world, but instead, they unwittingly have taken sides against them. Ateek referenced the woman in Lukes's account who stood before an unjust judge and cried out for justice for herself and against her oppressors. He utilizes the parable to describe the plight of the Palestinian struggle for justice in its pursuit of freedom and self-determination. Notice the following depiction by Ateek, where he also mentions the injustice of the colossal wall funded by the United States under the pretext of Israeli security:

The latest unjust mechanism exercised by Israel is the building of the monstrous wall, most of which snakes through Palestinian Land, in the face of international protests...There also seems to be a belief that if Israel increases its pressure on the Palestinians, it will succeed in driving them to despair so they will leave. There is also the belief that if Israel continues its violence, the Palestinians will react violently, giving Israel an excuse to justify killing them. This can serve as an excuse to terminate or interrupt any peace process, blame the Palestinians, and sustain the occupation...The cry of the widow is the cry of the Palestinians before the unjust judges of the government of Israel (Ateek 2008: 51).

Christian theology teaches us that earthly governments are ordained by God to preserve good and to deter evil, but never to inflict injustice against its citizens or their neighbors. When God allows a nation to exist, it is not for the purpose of enriching and preserving themselves, but to be a force for good. They are to do justice, love mercy and to walk humbly under God (Micah 6:8). Since the state of Israel is recognized as a legitimate nation in the world, it must be held to the same moral standards as all others. It should not be allowed to drive Palestinians out of their generational homes to preserve its national interests. The Old Testament conquest narratives are not given as instruction for how nations are to function today in fulfilling their greedy designs.

When people are dispossessed, dispersed and humiliated, not only with alleged divine support, but at the alleged express command of God, one's moral self-recoils in horror. Any association of God with the destruction of people must be subjected to an ethical analysis (Prior 1999: 11).

Christian theology teaches that Christ is the final word of instruction, and the mystery that had been hid for ages, not Old Testament narratives of conquest. Christ's words are final and practical instruction for his believers, which are too often ignored within Christian Zionism. Christ instructed his followers to love their enemies and promised blessings upon peacemakers. As Bishop Munib stated, *My Christ is not a warrior sent to kill and condemn but the Christ of the cross, who came to love and redeem all people (Younan 2007).* The theology that the world urgently needs is that of reconciliation, reparations and the equal dignity of all peoples, rather than the theology of war and political domination. It is true that the answers to peace in the Middle East are complicated. However, theological Zionism interferes with getting to those answers to peace and further complicates the conflict between the parties. It adds fuel to the flames of hostility, poisons the dialogue and diminishes the humanity of the image-bearers of God. It exacerbates racial conflict between those of European ancestry and ethnic groups that have long struggled for freedom.

Bishop Munib Younan explains why Christian Zionism is the very antithesis of the character of Jesus and is simply a continuation of the attributes that Christ demonstrated on Earth. He declares that *Christian Zionism tends to promote conflict and militarization rather than the biblical concepts of love, peace and nonviolence. In this theology, the gospel of is identified with the ideology of empire, colonialism and militarism* (Younan, 2007). Should diplomats around the world embrace Christian Zionism as its foundation for its Middle East policy, there is no room for Palestinian survival in their homeland. It is time for Christian Zionists to measure the correctness of their theology by the gospel of justice, liberation, and peace which Jesus Christ proclaimed.

5 THE THEOLOGY OF REPARATIONS

5.1 Compensation for Past Wrongs is Vital to Repairing and Reconciling Human Relationships

One of the most effective ways for two communities to repair their relationship, particularly if there is a history of violence, oppression or exploitation, is reparations. Reparations are a form of compensation on the part of the government or party responsible for damage inflicted or losses experienced, for those who have suffered unjustly. In some cases, financial compensation is given to those who have been directly impacted as well as indirectly impacted generationally by exploitation, genocide, slavery or displacement. Such compensation is not merely a legal remedy to resolve conflict but a theological ethic of justice and righteousness. Oftentimes, Christian theological writings and expression overemphasizes unconditional forgiveness and neglects the biblical ethic of restitution. In order to experience harmony and peace between societies with histories that need to be repaired, there must be acknowledgment of wrongs committed. After these wrongs are acknowledged, there must be a commitment on the part of the wrongdoer to repair the damage. Acknowledgment of transgressions must be specific in nature for understanding to occur. Love and forgiveness must be preceded by repentance, which is a commitment to change after having acknowledged the wrongs committed. Without this forgiveness and reconciliation becomes empty and temporary.

It is astonishing that Zionists advocate for compensation to Jews for the damages and suffering during the Holocaust, do not advocate the same for those who suffered as a result of the Trans-Atlantic Slavery Holocaust. No African country, black American population, Afro Caribbean nations, or Afro Latino population has been compensated for the ravages of the Slavery Holocaust. Many groups have received reparations for damages inflicted by powerful nations, such as the families of those of Japanese descent who unjustly suffered in prison camps in the U.S. during World

War II. If there is to be healing in the world, the United States, the most powerful in the world, can lead the way within its own borders. Christian theologians based in the United States should be at the forefront of pushing their legislators in the direction of reparations. This will display to the world that the United States has shifted toward justice and reconciliation and thus other nations will view America through a new lens. It will also provide a template for humility, repair, and reconciliations that other nations may follow.

5.2 Reparations for Historical Damages Have Precedence

Reparations for those who have suffered unjustly at the hands of oppressive governments and experienced loss through injustices have occurred throughout history. In recent history the United States government compensated Japanese Americans who were illegally detained during World War II due to fears they would be loyal to Japan. There were over 100,000, mainly United States citizens of Japanese ancestry who were forcibly removed from their home to be incarcerated under the name of national security. These actions by the U.S. government were later recognized as a violation of civil rights and an injustice against those of Japanese ancestry. These events created a greater level of awareness of crimes and thefts that had occurred among other population groups in the world and the need to repair the damage. Attention was also brought to the issue of slavery in the Americas and its generational impact. Demands for reparations due to slavery began to be made.

> *Brazil, Colombia, and Ecuador enacted new constitutions recognizing the right of land ownership for their black communities...The echoes of this movement were also heard in Africa, where a group of intellectuals, artists, politicians, and activists issued a document calling for reparations for the Atlantic slave trade and colonialism (Araujo 2017: 14).*

Most who fail to advocate for reparations for Africa and those of African ancestry in the Americas and in Europe, are not completely anti-reparations. Politically and socially active people in white society accept reparations for populations groups who have suffered theft at the hands of the state. This subject only becomes controversial when it comes to reparations for black people around the world. The gifting of Palestine to Jewish refugees because of the Holocaust and the ongoing funding of the state of Israel is a form of reparations, yet few protest it. There are Israeli citizens who have never been to Europe, nor have been directly impacted by the Holocaust, who benefit economically from reparations. The Transatlantic Enslavement Holocaust and Colonialist theft and slavery are not equally recognized. The Holocaust that the black race has suffered involved centuries of torture and brutality, but such history is often hidden. Reparations movements are not a new phenomenon; these efforts have existed for centuries and in some cases have been extremely fruitful.

> *But despite these [movements] to his day no former slave society in the Americas has paid restitutions to the descendants of slaves. Likewise, European countries have not paid financial reparations to their former colonies in the Americas, all of which, at least to some extent, relied on slave labor. Moreover, no African nation obtained any form of reparations for the Atlantic slave trade as well (Ibid., 15).*

No other people have suffered as much generational theft through slavery and colonialism than Africans and black people, yet these are most neglected and denied when considering restitution. Other groups who have not suffered as severely, have argued for and received reparations. A great proportion of the wealth and luxuries historically enjoyed by advanced industrialized societies are a direct result of the draining of its human and material resources. This reality cannot be overstated as it continues to this very day. Christian societies and organizations applaud themselves for their generous contributions to Africa, but these efforts in no way can equal the historic robbery of the continent. Foreign aid, as is currently constructed does not satisfy the historic debt owed to Africa and black people in the world. Some may suggest that slavery has always existed throughout the history of human civilization, and this is correct. However, Africans were the only ones who were enslaved based upon the color of their skin, with no legal recourse to escape and no rights as human beings. Entire generations were born into slavery and never tasted freedom at any point in their lives. Husbands, wives, and children were separated at the public auction, and sold alongside livestock. They were not only robbed of their freedom, but also language, culture, history, and dignity. The severity and harshness of the slavery holocaust is unparalleled in history.

5.3 Slavery and Colonialism Were Exercises in Generational Theft

Oftentimes western literature portrays the enslavement society they created, as a legitimate civic structure. The slavery system is often colored as a sometimes cruel but overall, a necessary evil to create a prosperous world. The death camps where the enslaved labored are given the softer name of plantations. The human traffickers and kidnappers who bought, sold and owned the enslaved are given sanitized titles such as landowners and aristocrats. Among the enslaved black people, there were a significant portion of women who were rape victims. Rather than referring to them as rape victims, they are referred to by the title of mistresses. The whitewashed view of European history and the colonial period has created the impression that Black holocaust period was humane and bearable. The total inhumanity of this holocaust is not appreciated. In too many cases, the animals who lived in the white kidnapper's death camps ate better than the enslaved.

> *Slavery existed in most world societies since antiquity. It took different forms in various times and places. Yet, several societies where slavery existed, at least to some extent, recognized slaves as human beings (Ibid., 23).*

One reaction to the call for reparations for the descendants of slaves in the Americas is to question why this has suddenly become a public appeal. The reality is that the petition for reparations has always existed, but consistently and persistently ignored. The call for reparations for the descendants of slavery did not begin in the twenty-first century. Those who suffered from the chains of slavery understood their condition was an injustice and demanded compensation for their backbreaking labor in the cotton fields. The enslaved were quite conscious that their ancestors were kidnapped and taken from a foreign land. They realized that they were treated unjustly by being held in chains and forced to live an inferior existence under the control of their kidnappers. Aware that humans who labor and create wealth are deserving of compensation, they demanded reparations from the very beginning. A contemporary during the era of abolitionist Fredrick Douglass was a freedom fighter by the name of Martin Delany. Delaney blazed a significant trail for the cause of reparations in 1854. Delany was born a freedman and an outspoken advocate for abolition and equal rights for black people. His advocacy occurred well before the American Civil War and the subsequent Emancipation Proclamation of U.S. President Abraham Lincoln. At a convention in 1854, he declared the following concerning reparations for what he described as "unparalleled wrongs."

"Nothing less than a national indemnity, indelibly fixed by virtue of our own sovereign potency, will satisfy us as a redress of grievances for the unparalleled wrongs, undisguised impositions, and unmitigated oppression, which we have suffered at the hands of this American people (Ibid., 63)."

Another reality that often goes unmentioned is the socio-economic conditions of formerly enslaved people immediately following emancipation. For over two-hundred years, the enslaved population in the United States never owned land or property but were considered the property of Whites. Although millions rejoiced in their newly found freedom, they were homeless people with no place to call home. Justice and human decency would have demanded that the new free people be rewarded with financial, and material means for their survival. Though promises were made, they were never put into action. Enslaved people were forced to find food and shelter under the most impoverished conditions. Children of families suffered from hunger and were exposed to harsh weather conditions with no recourse from the government or business community. At no point did those in civic leadership or lawmaking positions consider the plight of new freepersons who struggled to survive. They received no assistance from those who contributed to their enslavement. Leader of the U.S. civil rights movement of the 1950s and 60s, Reverend Martin Luther King advocated for reparations to assist the descendants of the enslaved. King recalled the history of those black Americans who were incarcerated in privatized U.S. labor camps as enslaved persons, were not compensated after freedom. In his book, *Where do we Go from Here*, King referenced the experiences of the over four million free people who left their incarcerated state with no food, land or shelter for their survival, and the injustice of such a state.

> *It was like freeing a man who had been unjustly imprisoned for years, and on discovering his innocence sending him out with no bus fare to get home, no suit to cover his body, no financial compensation to atone for his long years of incarceration (King 1967: 86-87).*

The injustice of withholding compensation for their labor and long unjust incarceration is compounded by the fact that the white majority in the U.S., following the Civil War were given free land. These land grants were not given as a form of compensation to white farmers, but as gifts to help expand the United States territory further west. These events occurred while America's new freepersons were left to the elements to survive on their own. The act of granting free land to the white citizens of America was evidence that indeed the same could have and should be done for its black citizens. This granting of land to white farmers gave them a level of security, real estate and wealth to past down to their progenitors. Moreover, the children of enslaved people who labored for free for generations were never given any real estate for the exploitation of their labor. As a result, they possessed nothing to pass down to the coming generations as did their white counterparts. This is the history of why there exists today, so many inequities between the white and black American citizens. A fewer proportion of black Americans are land or homeowners compared to whites. Such a social condition should not exist in a nation that built its prosperity from the involuntary labor camps embraced by the U.S economic and legal systems.

> *Presently, the group to which I belong is a bottom caste in*

> *American society. This, in fact, has always been the place we were made to occupy. And for every dollar that whites possess, ADOS hold only ten cents. Not surprisingly—since society is always eager to justify inequality by assigning defects to the victims of inequality rather than to the system that produces it (Cosby 2021: 24).*

A cultural idiom in the United States says, "Every person should pull themselves up by their own bootstraps" rather than receiving help from the community or the government. What is often overlooked is that reparations are not "giving" something away to a person or population group, but it is an act of restorative justice. It is an attempt, as far as feasibly possible to repair what has been generationally stolen. Simultaneously, while calling upon the black race to lift themselves up without assistance, white citizens were given free land and an economic base. Partiality and racism are not overt in the American protestant "bootstrap" theology, but subtly contributes to a discriminatory mindset. Dr. Martin Luther King Jr. referred to this injustice. It is true that many black citizens of America as well as immigrants indeed pulled themselves out of poverty, but such miracles do not release a society from the exercise of justice and the restoration of what has been stolen. If a person steals money from a person, the fact that they survived does not release the thief from the obligation of returning it. It is often the case that white Christian theologian refer to Dr. King's message of unity, which they seek to fulfill by forgetting the past. While focusing on unity they fail to make not of his prophetic speech concerning the justice of reparations.

> *After the war the government granted white settlers, without cost, millions of acres of land in the West, thus providing America's new white peasants from Europe with an economic floor. But at the same time its oldest peasantry, the Negro, was denied everything but a legal status he could not use, could not consolidate, could not even defend (King 1967: 86-87).*

Reverend Martin Luther King Jr comes from an extensive line of Christian clergy who advocated for reparations on behalf of black

Americans. Advocacy for reparations were included in the religious dialogue, sermons and publications of both white and black abolitionists during the slavery period of American history. Contemporary Christian theologians rarely touch upon the horrors of the Trans-Atlantic Slave Holocaust, much less advocate for reparations.

5.4 Beneficiaries from the Legacy of Slavery and Colonialism are Responsible for Reparations as Heirs

A sizable portion mainstream theologians believe that the present generation is not responsible for crimes committed against the ancestors of black Americans, and that black people should not dwell in the past. A great proportion believe that black Americans should forgive, forget and seek unity with their white counterparts. They fail to uphold the theological ethic of confession, repentance and restitution as the prerequisites for reconciliation and unity. A massive portion of clergyman during the slavery era in the United States believed in the theology of reparations and that compensation and repair must done for the black American community. If Western Christianity is to have a respected voice with moral weight and substance in the world, it must return to this theological ethic of reparations. This ethic answers the question of what must be done regarding returning what has been stolen by *white supremacist theft* in a multigenerational sense. This answer involves both repentance and restoration (Kwon and Thompson 2021: 163).

If the United States can bring about racial harmony within its own nation, then certainly it would be listened to when it comes to solving conflicts around the world. If the Western church is to lead the way in bringing warring factions together and work for peace and harmony among the nations, it must lead the way by charting a path to restorative justice within its own borders. It is true that the Western church has a theological heritage that led to expansionism, genocide and human enslavement, but the heritage of abolitionism which held the moral high ground of history. It is the latter tradition that the Western church must align in order to set the example of reconciliation and ethnic harmony. Those theologians of the West, who argue against reparations since the current generation is not responsible for actions of one's ancestors, contradict the biblical ethic of restitution. According to Numbers 5:8, restitution belongs to both the owner of stolen goods as well as their descendants, heirs, children and those with family connections (Ibid., 173). The property still belongs to the family that has been robbed even if the heirs of the stolen goods did not personally commit the robbery.

Nebuchadnezzar, who later became king, was the top general in the Babylonian army when Jerusalem was besieged in 597 BC. However, neither Nebuchadnezzar nor his progenitors were ruling when the decree for reparations for the Jews was signed by Cyrus of the Persian realm (Ezra 1:1-6 NIV). The Persian government did not directly inflict any damages upon the Jews and Jerusalem, but they realize that they were the beneficiaries of the religious and societal theft committed by the Babylonians. The neighbors of the Jews were not cause the damage that the Babylonians caused, but they too were beneficiaries. The reparations must come from those who inherited stolen wealth and given from those who were generationally deprived of it. In fact, the decree of Cyrus had been forgotten, and later recovered by King Darius, and the orders of that decree were to be set in motion. Funding for the reparations were to be taken from the King's treasury revenues, which were similar to today's system of taxation. Not only were the funds to be released on behalf of the Jews, but the neighbors in the areas where they lived were to assist them in the journey. They were to receive livestock, gold, silver and whatever they needed. They were to be fully funded. It would be a crime for local rulers or the Jew's neighbors to interfere with their ability to move, gain compensation and assistance (Ezra 6:6-12 NIV). They were not permitted to complain and say "We are not responsible because the damage occurred under a different king, under a different reign, and we did not personally cause the damage that Nebuchadnezzar had inflicted. We were not alive during that time, and those receiving the payment were not alive nor directly affected by Nebuchadnezzar's siege. Why should we bear the burden of assisting them? Why should the monies contributed to the king's treasury be utilized fund Israel's return when there are other pressing needs?" Such claims and evasiveness would not be permitted or countenanced in a just and equitable society.

5.5 Compensation for Past Wrongs are not Charitable Gifts but Debts to be Paid

One of the arguments against reparations by both black and white Christians is that black people are not as good at managing monies as their white counterparts, and therefore it would be a waste. This mindset suggests that restitution must not be given unless the community that has been robbed can prove they are worthy of the wealth distributed. This mindset is quite revealing. It suggests that white society does not really believe that anything has been stolen, and that reparations have more to do with charity than justice. When one recognizes that something has been stolen, they do not consider whether the victim is savvy enough to handle what belongs to them. They simply return it. Even if white America emptied out its national treasury for the purposes of reparations, it still would not equal the amount that has been robbed. Most white Christians do not recognize the level of theft and economic rape that has occurred, and that the United State government is eternally indebted to black America due the crimes against humanity occurring during the slavery holocaust. When one understands the colossal theft that occurred, one's love for humanity will never ask whether one deserves what has been stolen from them.

It is not the business of white society to concern themselves with how reparations monies will be used. It does not belong to them but to those who have been robbed. A robber does not concern himself with how the owner will utilize his own goods once he returns them. This mindset suggests that white society believes that what was taken was rightfully stripped away by those who had the superior mental acumen to manage it. This comes from an unwitting desire to continue illegal ownership of what rightfully belongs to black America. Theologian, Duke Kwon views this thinking as a problematic desire to control what belongs to the robbed. The following statement exposes both the problem and the inconsistency of such thinking. Whites may view themselves as morally superior in the management of wealth, but the fact that reparations are even necessary proves otherwise. Slavery was itself both an illegal transfer of wealth from one race to another based on the assumed superiority of those of European ancestry. Whites do not have the moral high ground as it relates to the ethical and judicious use of wealth by other races. Therefore, if black America will misuse wealth, it is itself the same prejudice that created the need for reparations. When White immigrant settlers were given land and treasure to prosper in the United States, no one questioned whether they would squander or misuse it. When the state of Israel was given Palestine, no one questioned whether they would misuse it.

> As Anasa Troutman pointedly puts it, "If your concern is 'What if black people spend the money unwisely?' you are living in white supremacy...And that happens in every economic transaction every day everywhere in the world, including those made by white folks (Ibid., 247).

The debt that is owed to black America is not only due to slavery but also the discriminatory and oppressive actions that followed. Even though the argument that slavery was so long ago is invalid, there are successive crimes against black America that continued after slavery. These crimes include terrorists lynching and subsequent displacement by black homeowners, denial of admission to colleges and universities, and the exploitation of black famers. Other examples might include black codes which led to mass imprisonment and a return to labor camps for the smallest violations. Additionally, it may also include the consignment to second class citizenship due to Jim Crow laws, which led to a lack of opportunities and economic limitations. Finally, it may also involve the bombing and burning down of prosperous black towns and cities in the 1920s. The debt that is owed certainly begins with slavery, but it assuredly does not end there. Indeed, the debt is immeasurable. Those who fail to recognize the depth of the debt often assign blame to black America for the economic suffering that exists due to their own decision making within the culture. Reverend Kevin Cosby, MDiv., uses the acronym ADOS in referring to black Americans. ADOS stands for American descendants of Slavery. Cosby argues that of all population groups in the United States, none have experience to the level of theft as ADOS. In spite of this theft which created the significant disparity between white and black, many white Christians deny that the plight of black America has a connection to the oppressive policies of America's history. Dr. King addressed the racist and classist prejudice against the poor. He said, *the poor are less often dismissed from our conscience today by being branded as inferior and incompetent* (King 1967: 162). The poor are not criminals as they are often portrayed and do not always exist due to bad choices but rather the exploitative practices of a racist and economically unjust capitalist system. Poverty is often criminalized and demonized in capitalistic systems. It is the systems themselves that are criminal rather than the poor. These systems have criminally exploited black America for centuries. Those decisions made by a white supremacist society were not merely bad choices but evil actions. It is the west that became rich through evil actions rather than the marginalized becoming poor through bad choices. Reverend Cosby further adds:

> *But in fact that utter absence of wealth within ADOS is more appropriately understood as a direct result of centuries of draconian, often state-sanctioned practices that specifically exploited and excluded us. The reality, then, is that it has never been about the choices that ADOS make but about the choices that ADOS have (Cosby 2021: 24).*

In various places in the world, those generations who were directly harmed have passed and those immediately affected economically and culturally are no longer alive. In some cases, promised compensation for damages was never rewarded. This does not eliminate the responsibility of those who have enjoyed the prosperity stemming from generational exploitation. Those who benefited from prior generations of exploiters should support the idea of compensating those who descended from the exploited. Such compensation acknowledges both the wrongs committed and it honors the humanity of those who have suffered loss. Those who argue against reparations point to those of the present generation and say that they were not around when the damage initially occurred. They add that their generation should not be responsible for the damage inflicted by their ancestors who lived long ago. These ideas are advanced by Christian theologians who emphasize individual responsibility over societal responsibility. This impacts the thinking of mainstream Christians. Christian theology, however, emphasizes both individual as well as societal responsibility. Not only are individuals judged by Divinity, but also nations and communities. Concepts that suggest that one is only culpable for actions that one has directly committed are erroneous. Societies to which one belongs are also responsible if indeed it has benefited from damage it has caused to others. Repair is the root word for reparations. That one should fix what one has broken is a universal principle. It applies not only to individuals but nations. Wherever societies have been broken by the powerful governments, it is the duty of those powerful governments to fix what has been broken. The idea that one is not personally responsible because it predated their existence is irrelevant. This manner of justifying societal neglect may be refuted by what may be described as the Ezra principle that is given in the scriptures by that name.

5.6 The European Colonial Powers are Indebted to the African and other Black Nations for the History of Slavery and Colonialism

Reparations for the descendants of slavery in the United States is only one microcosm of international indebtedness owed to African and Caribbean nations and other formerly enslaved and colonized societies. Haiti is a prime example of this. It was the first enslaved population in the Americas to overthrow their enslavers and to become independently free. Fifty thousand black people died in the struggle, yet it is ironic that the French demanded that the Haitian nation, of humans who were enslaved and tortured by them. It was demanded that they pay reparations to the enslaver empire of France for fighting for their own humanity and freedom. Considering this reality, not only does France owe the Haitians reparations for their enslavement, but also the continued exploitation following independence.

> *Haiti agreed to pay reparations to France in order to gain international recognition. The sum was fixed by treaty at 150 million francs. The Haitian economy was bled by these payments, which were not completed until 1922. The French government, then, imposed 97 years of financial burden upon the infant state (Milwood 2012: 53).*

Imagine on practical level, a human being kidnapped, who then must compensate the kidnapper due to their efforts to assert their humanity and escape their kidnapper. This is exactly what occurred between the French and the Haitians. The legacy of slavery and the subsequent exploitation of the Haitians has caused the first independent black nation in the western hemisphere the poorest in the world. Trillions are owed to Haiti. It is one of the poorest not because of the practice of voodoo (a common Christian myth and stereotype,) but because they have been cruelly and severely robbed of their wealth and have never been compensated for their generational servitude to France. When Haitian leaders began to cry out for respect and recognition as equally human through a campaign for reparations, the reactions by France and the US were harsh.

> *President Aristide placed a formal request to the French government [for reparations,] who denounced him, and in association with the United States, moved speedily to remove him from office in order to counter the reparations claim. But the movement continues as a part of the 21st century stage in the struggle against the Transatlantic Slave Trade (Ibid., 53).*

No European president nor prime minister would be treated in such a way for simply demanding what was rightfully owed. Reparations to Haiti, is difficult for white countries to accept because it would be an acknowledgment by France, that the revolution of the enslaved was morally justified. This requires confession and humility on the part of the French, which many great powers struggle to accept. They do not want to seem as though they are bowing to an inferior, but Jesus taught that the greatest amongst us are those who are willing to become servant. Also, they fear those reparations to Haiti, will give strong voice to the cause of reparations in the US and black nations around the world. Arrogance and misguided illusions of superiority will never drown out the cries for economic and social liberation. No one is absolutely free until all are free.

> *The power and presence of Jesus gives the community of black people the freedom and power to say to Europe, Britain, and America that God's Kingdom is bound up with the Pan-African and continental Pan-African demand for reparation. Without an unequivocal apology and comprehensive reparation, justice, freedom, reconciliation, liberty, and equality will be an epistemological dream. (Ibid., 81).*

Christian theologians, clergypersons, and charitable organizations would rather approach Haiti and Africa from a humanitarian sense through distribution of clothing, food and building of houses, than call for justice and restitution. These efforts to serve the needs of the poor should be commended but such charity does not solve the root of the problem which is the history of free labor and economic exploitation. Blacks and Africans would not need such charity if the cry for justice is answered. When the call for reparations is answered, it may provide a standard for reconciliation and international cooperation between the exploiter and the exploited wherever this dynamic exists in the world. When the exploiter displays humility through its actions, it frees other exploiters to see the benefits and follow such examples. Additionally, it eliminates the historical stains of the past. However, nations should not compensate for their past crimes for the sake of selfish benefit, but because it is right. This will heal the wounds of the past and eliminate the stain of those who caused such wounds. Many of the conflicts in Haiti and Africa have a direct connection to the poverty, competition for meager resources and the powerlessness that has been inflicted upon them due to generational theft. Such remedies will aid in helping alleviate the poverty that has been forced upon them, which in turn will minimize violent actions between competing tribes and political parties.

The European powers must acknowledge that the "Jesus" that they represented in their efforts to "civilize" and reorder the world, to which they attribute their "blessings," is a false idol that should be dismantled and demolished for the true Jesus of compassion, liberty and restoration. This work of repentance and renunciation of such an idol is also required in order to remove the bloodstain from the hands of the great powers. Milwood expresses this reality in no uncertain terms. The Christ of Nazareth and Galilee demonstrated his righteous anger toward exploiters by overturning the money-changers tables in Jerusalem and charging them with extortion and thievery. The true Jesus of Christian theology abhors manipulation, exploitation and generational theft. He demands justice, healing and restitution. He condemns those who have made *his father's house* (in this case the world which he owns) *a den of thieves (Matthew 21:13)*. Since generational thievery against Africa and its descendants has occurred, as in the case of Zaccheus of the gospels, repayment above and beyond is urgent and imperative. Without such actions, the stain remains, and the moral voice of Western nations must be questioned.

> *The transatlantic chattel slave trade in Africans cannot be obliterated as a flagitious (a stain on the character of Britain, Europe, and America) until full reparation is made to Africa for the heinous crime of enslavement of its people in the name of their white cultural- semantic Christianity of God and Jesus Christ (Ibid., 81).*

Confession and humility on the part of the world's great powers may also encourage disputing parties within other nations to find paths of reconciliation that the world desperately needs. It is time for the world's great powers to cease blaming developing nations for their problems and confess to their historic and current role in creating those problems. It is true that formerly colonized people are not blameless, but much of the brokenness that exists is due to generational thievery. When the most powerful nations of the world recognize the full humanity and dignity of the generationally disenfranchised and exploited populations, it is then that the great work of reconciliation on Earth can begin. Reparations are a critical aspect of achieving peace and social harmony.

Justice for the historically oppressed in the form of reparations cannot be a one-time action. It must be a long term and ongoing commitment to address historic thievery. In the aftermath of World War II, many Western European nations were capitals and cities were devastated and demolished. The infrastructure, such as buildings, roads and bridges, was either damaged or reduced to rubble. Rebuilding Europe would take several years. The United States government, even though they were not responsible for the devastation of Europe, allocated resources to rebuild European cities. If the U.S., who had nothing to do with destroying British cities, implemented policies for its rebuilding, certainly such a campaign would be appropriate and just in the case of an aggressive plan for the development of Africa, black America, and other former European colonies. The European nations were given major assistance for its rebuilding with nothing expected in return, yet any assistance toward Africa is often attached to expectations. Western governments must not see Africa as weak and in need of charity, but as eternally in debt to Africans and the formerly colonized peoples. Dr. Martin Luther King Jr. Pointed out that the debt owed to Africa should be similar to the Marshall Plan implemented for Europe and should be far greater and more sustained. A period of twenty years was recommended by King. As such a "Marshall Plan" is implemented, Westerners should avoid paternalism and control. He expressed that such a sustained campaign is not only just but also achievable (King 1967: 176).

When Christian theologians in the US no longer ignore, minimize, or erase the historical impact of slavery, and join in the cause of restitution and reconciliation, it may provide a moral standard for Europeans to also respect the humanity of African nations by returning to them the true value for the export of its raw materials, supporting a system that encourages not just the export of raw materials but fully developed goods and as well as reparations for colonialism. It may provide a legal standard which may prove to be a deterrent for such crimes against humanity in the future.

5.7 Conclusion: Reparations Blazes a Trail for Restorative Justice Around the World

Should Western theologians push their democracies in the direction of humility, confession, restitution, and reconciliation, rather than domination and expansionism in the world, the trail for peace and harmony will be blazed. Such a movement may inspire healing and reconciliation in the Middle East, and a resolution for the displaced refugee status of millions of Palestinians may be resolved. In fact, Alex Walker, when considering the Palestinian plight, said that reminded her of what it was like *being black and living in the United States under American-style apartheid and the daily insults to one's sense of being human* (Makdisi 2010: 18). It is indeed a shared struggle for God-given dignity and to reclaim one's rightful inheritance. Reparations in America and other responsible nations will doubtless inspire hope for what is possible. Additionally, it may provide a template to fix what is broken and lessen the economic distance between oppressed and oppressor along with increasing international goodwill. When nations around the world, which have been historically robbed by the great powers, are socially and economically restored, this may in many cases eliminate the causes of conflict. Many of the conflicts and civil wars in the world, particularly in Latin America have their roots in the scarcity created by systemic theft of resources brought about by both historic and neocolonialism.

> *The persistence into the twentieth century of a specific institutional pattern inimical to growth in Mexico and Latin America is well illustrated by the fact that, just as in the nineteenth century, the pattern generated economic stagnation and political instability, civil wars and coups, as groups struggled for the benefits of power. (Acemoglu and Robinson 2012: 38).*

When nations are committed to restorative justice, conflicts would be lessened between poorer factions, living in a state of scarcity and desperate for survival and economic security. The world would come much closer to peace, reconciliation and social harmony. It is not the suggestion of this chapter that monetary reparations are the only way to restore and heal. Reparations might also include restoring of land, compensation through land grants, government funded rebuilding of communities, commitment to infrastructure development or free access to education.

Rather than invading countries in order to fight terrorism, restorative justice on the part of the great powers will create a world order where its appeal and influence is greatly reduced and diminished. Instead of investing in the building of private prisons and excessive policing African American communities, reparations will move millions out of poverty, where crime is less appealing. Other studies might be conducted by sociologists to discover creative ways to address restoration based on singular issues which are applicable to local situations. The post-World War II Marshall Plan for rebuilding Europe remains a template in this regard. Such actions would not be an act of charity or a handout, but simply an act of justice and righting historical wrongs.

Dr. Eric Betts

6 THE URGENT NEED FOR COMMUNITY AND HUMAN COMMONALITY

6.1 Reconciliation is a cornerstone of Christian Theology

Reconciliation is a foundational pillar in Christian theology because it deals with the purpose what Jesus came to accomplish both in his life and in his death. There are three questions that must be answered as it relates to reconciliation. What is reconciliation from a theological perspective? Why is it necessary? What impact does this form of reconciliation have upon community? Evangelical theologian, Charles Ryrie defines reconciliation, which is accomplished on Jesus' cross, as the following:

> *Reconciliation means a change of relationship from hostility to harmony and peace between two parties. People can be reconciled to each other (Matt. 5:24, diallasso; 1 Cor. 7:11, katallasso), and people have been reconciled to God (Rom. 5:1–11; 2 Cor. 5:18–21, katallasso; Eph. 2:16; Col. 1:20, apokatallasso)... Because of sin...Our state of estrangement [from God] could not have been more serious, nor the need for a change, a reconciliation, more urgent (Ryrie 1999: 337).*

It must be understood that the reconciliation that Christ brought about was not merely reversing human beings' estrangement from the divine, but also estrangement from each other. This is important because we all bear the image of God. How can one be reconciled to God and yet be estranged from his image-bearers. Humans were originally designed to live together in harmony. *God is reconciled to [humanity], [humanity] is reconciled to God, both are reconciled to each other (ibid., 337).*

It is vital that theologians, Christian leaders, and clergy emphasize more strongly the need for reconciliation among the family of humanity. One cannot discuss reconciliation without discussing what has brought about alienation which is sin. Racism, exploitation, injustice, violence, and oppression are sin. Too often theologians focus on individual sins toward God and each other where it relates to reconciliation, but there are also societal/governmental sins. This also estranges people from each other. Societal sins must be dealt with in the spirit of Christ and his cross in order to reverse the estrangement. Human beings' attitudes toward one another from a societal standpoint reveals that societies attitude about Christ.

> *Yet though the world has been reconciled, man needs to be reconciled by changing his position about Christ. Then, and only then, is his condition before God changed (ibid., 339).*

When Ryrie writes about reconciliation through changing one's position about Christ, he means the person of Christ. However, it is important to understand that whatever attitudes or acts are committed by a dominant group against another group further down in the social hierarchy, is the same as being manifested toward Christ himself. Christ in addressing the nations stated that, whatever is done to *the least of these is also done to me* (Matt. 25:40). Therefore, changing one's position about Christ for the purposes of reconciliation, involves changing one's position toward those regarded as the least in society. The late Howard Thurman was a theologian, philosopher and civil rights leader who served as dean of Rankin Chapel at Howard University. His words in his famous book, Jesus and the Disinherited shows the sacred importance of reconciliation and valuing human dignity. He states, *A [person's] conviction that he is God's child automatically tends to shift the basis of his relationship with all his fellows. He recognizes at once that to fear a man, whatever may be that man's power over him, is a basic denial of the integrity of his very life* (Thurman 1976: 40-41). Jemar Tisby is a Christian historian on race and religion, who is also a bestselling author. Tisby has found that evangelicals have in some cases confessed to their sordid history on its treatment of black people and by extension non-whites, but he states that their standard for what reconciliation means does not go far enough. He uses the 1995 Southern Baptist Convention as an example:

> *In 1995, the Southern Baptist Convention, the largest protestant denomination in the United States and one that was founded to preserve the so-called right of White Christians to hold slaves, finally repented of its racist origins. They passed a resolution on racial reconciliation...But racial reconciliation as it is popularly understood and practiced in Evangelical Chrisitan circles suffers from three main shortcomings: it misdiagnoses the problem as 'separation,' it does not properly address power dynamics, and it does not take gender into consideration (Tisby 2021: 101)*

Any structures, institutions or philosophies adopted by a society that creates estrangement is contrary to the cross and what Jesus came to accomplish. This is what Evangelical theology must recognize and it is a cross they must be willing to bear. They cannot leave it to the oppressed to work alone in this endeavor for liberation. Merely hugging and shaking hands gives the illusion of reconciliation but it does not exist without justice and restoration. The historic civil right leader Rev. Jesse Jackson. was interviewed by Greg Arnold in an issue of *Christianity Today* in 1977. In the article Jackson made a profound statement about difference between the late, and historic evangelist Rev. Billy Graham and the Rev. Dr. Martin Luther King Jr. The statement created quite a metaphor for the problem of Evangelical shortcomings on reconciliation. Jackson noted that Billy Graham, if he had lived in Moses' day, would have preached to the souls of the Hebrew slaves in Egypt, and afterwards would have sent them back to the mud-pits to work. Jackson further added, Graham would have after preaching to the Hebrew slaves would have afterwards played golf with Pharoah. Martin Luther King Jr., on the other hand, according to Jackson, would have mingled with the Hebrew slaves, and afterwards he would have preached judgment to Pharoah and demanded that the Hebrew slaves be set free. He would have risked his life doing so (Christianity Today, 1977). Graham, in this metaphor, would represent the common Evangelical view of reconciliation. Martin Luther King's representation in this metaphor is reflective of Jesus' view of a holistic reconciliation.

6.2 Selective reconciliation for political reasons fails to bring healing

The legacy of the racial tensions in the United States has much to do with selective reconciliation. During the American Civil War, where the southern states broke away from the Union in order to preserve slavery, and the northern states fought to preserve the union, the nation was severely fractured. Anger and resentment due to the competing politics between free states and slave states led to this fracturing. Hundreds of thousands on both sides perished in the war. Following the war, practical efforts on part of the United States government were made in order to reconcile the north and the south post-civil war for the success of the Union. What was overlooked was the needful reconciliation of the enslavers toward the enslaved, because there was little political or structural benefit for such. In fact, while the south and the north were reconciling, societal lines of separation were being drawn between blacks and whites. The reconciliation that Christian theology envisions involves more than reconciliation only for convenient political purposes. It reaches all peoples and all that separates, because the cross does not discriminate nor selectively reconcile.

> *White Christians who were formerly devoted to abolition placed more emphasis on sectional reconciliation than on the continuing fight against White supremacy. And so it was, from Reconstruction through the Jim Crow era, the story of the church's faithful resistance against White supremacy was carried by and large by African American Christians (Kwon and Thompson 2021: 135).*

Ignoring and overlooking the true reconciliation which would come at a higher cost, has led to much racial hostility and estrangement in the United States in its subsequent history. It should not have been the burden of the oppressed to fight for reconciliation, but those who have committed the historical wrongs which led to social fracturing. Such reconciliation would have led to White America losing its status on the social hierarchy chain and was viewed as too high a price. However, who can estimate the price a society has paid when its most talented members are locked out so many years from participating. The same can be said of nations in the world who conveniently reconcile for political advantage by forming alliances with former enemies. Reconciliation must be genuine and non-discriminatory in order to usher in the kind of world Jesus envisioned.

6.3 Reconciliation begins where Western arrogance ends

Reconciliation is achievable only if the strongest in the world are willing to come down from the hills of superiority and hear the grievances of the oppressed. The great powers and their societies must be willing to be made uncomfortable as they hear about how they are perceived among the exploited populations of the world. The western world has been misguided and lacks self-awareness about the role they play on the world stage. Many have been conditioned to believe that because of their claims of democracy, the successes of World War II, their role in the fall of communism, and foreign aid, that they are a moral force for good in the world. The citizens of the world powers are shielded from many of the atrocities that are committed in the world by their governments. They recognize that their governments have made mistakes, but see those mistakes as outweighed by the good that they have done. They also view any evil that is committed by their governments as necessary evils. They see colonialism as having somewhat of a negative impact but view those negatives as necessary to civilize the world and unite the continents by European languages. Slavery may be seen by them as unavoidable in helping to build a nation that would be a moral and economic force in the world. In a sense, many western leaders and citizenry are blind to the daily realities that exist outside of their population groups. They are oblivious to the suffering that exists in the world because of economic exploitation and political manipulation at the hands of their governments. In order to further complete the "ministry of reconciliation," humility must be the core principle with which Western powers should operate. Humility requires the capacity to listen and learn about the plight of others and how to help alleviate their pain. Self-justification, defensive postures, excuses and finger pointing must be surrendered in order to begin the process of reconciliation. Dr. Martin Luther King chastises the attitude of Westerners as being unaware of their superiority complex that causes them to feel that they have so much with which to educate the world rather than believing that they may have the need of being educated by others. *The Western arrogance of feeling that it has everything to teach others and nothing to learn from them is not just* (King 1967: 184). Such willingness to listen and learn on the part of Western leaders and their citizenry must be genuine and sincere.

This process of learning must be deliberate, compassionate, practical and sustained. It must be seen as necessary for the survival and progress of the human race. Dr. King refers to this lack of education on the part of Whites becomes a barrier to community and human relationships. He adds, *Whites, it must frankly be said, are not putting in a similar mass effort to reeducate themselves out of their racial ignorance* (Ibid., 24). Humility that leads to reconciliation requires painstaking maximum effort and large-scale undertaking to correct four hundred years of ignorance and miseducation. Humility is not the end of the process of reconciliation on the Earth, but a full acceptance and acknowledgment of the wrongs that have been committed. This means repentance and renunciation of the past must occur. Such acknowledgement may mean that the aggrieved may advise remedies to former crimes that may not be in the immediate political or economic interest of the West.

> *The West must enter into the program with humility and penitence and a sober realization that everything will not always "go our way." It cannot be forgotten that the Western powers were but yesterday the colonial masters (Ibid., 176).*

Reconciliation and ethnic harmony are often spoken of in terms that absolves former colonial powers of any responsibility for the crimes against humanity that have been committed. This is true not only in secular circles but also religious ones. The attitudes and language of the great powers is one where those in power demand the terms of reconciliation. Interpretations of reconciliation often ignore or do not appreciate the level generational pain, torture, trauma, suffering and depravation that has occurred as a result of the greed and inhumane actions of history. Additionally, the burden of the struggle for reconciliation on the part of Europeans should be as vigorous as the struggle of oppressed people for liberation. The oppressed people of the world should not need to both bear the struggle for liberation as well as reconciliation. The burden should rest primarily on those who have created a world of brokenness, devastation, and disunity. European powers should not assume that they understand what reconciliation means. For oppressed groups to answer the call of reconciliation by the great powers of the world, without meeting the criteria would be a crime against the coming generations who deserve to leave in peace and fulfillment. According to Professor James Cone, those who desire reconciliation should consult the poorer nations and populations concerning the meaning of reconciliation and not the poor agreeing to reconciliation based on historical white interpretations. Cone argues that Eurocentric influence and historical context of exploitation and inhumanity somewhat blinds the minds of Western powers to the realities of the struggles of those fighting for human dignity. He suggests that Western ideas of reconciliation are shaped by views of their own superiority and privilege, and that European power should be self-aware of these blind spots. Cone adds that Western ideas of reconciliation are oftentimes self-serving and based on desires for the oppressed to simply state that they do not wish them any ill will concerning past injustices.

> *[Too often] whites view reconciliation as promises not to commit future injustices, while the oppressed will open the door to new relations based on such promises...Reconciliation is not a sentimental feeling of goodwill but a hard-fought struggle to reach a new era of justice, harmony and mutual respect (Cone 1997: 353).*

Far too often Evangelical's do not recognize their responsibilities before Christ as it relates to restorative justice. Restorative justice is included in the reconciliation Jesus envisioned. They must admit that this too is a major aspect of Jesus' ministry and the gospel he preached. Reconciliation must involve love and love never leaves its neighbor in a state of disrepair. This is especially true when one's organization was a part of causing the disrepair.

6.4 Reconciliation imagines war as an outdated method of resolving conflict in this advanced scientific age

Throughout the history of the human race, old hostilities, greedy expansionism, competing interests and competition for resources have been the cause of war. War was a mechanism to solve conflicts where the strongest flourished and controlled their futures. The problem with war is that it devalues human life and dignity, and places national or ethnic goals above respect for human dignity. Moreover, it devalues the interdependence of various societies and diverse populations. War destroys human life which is divinely given. No human can give life and therefore have no right to destroy life. Oftentimes in today's world, war hawks often speak of avoiding civilian casualties, yet this remains an unintended side effect to war. It cuts off supply chains which leads to hunger, starvation, and outbreaks of disease. After weeks, months and years of fighting, brutal wars eventually end. In most cases, wars end with dialogue between the two sides and disputes are settled. The question then arises, "why not avoid the loss of human life and begin the dialogue before peace unravels, when dialogue will eventually occur?" War appears as simply a means to postpone dialogue and delay the diplomatic process. Such a posture is too immeasurably costly to justify. King calls for a "revolution of values" that will view was as an inhumane way of solving disputes. Additionally, he calls for a reordering of priorities.

> *A true revolution of values will lay hands on the world order and say of war: "This way of settling differences is not just." ... A nation that continues year after year to spend more money on military defense than on programs of social uplift is approaching spiritual death (King 1967: 184).*

As King recognizes that war is unjust, it continues to be a human reality because it remains profitable. Justice and peace do not appear as profitable as militarism. Dehumanization always occurs when profit is placed above the theological reality of what it means to be a human being in the image of God. If the human being were truly valued as creation and the cross of Jesus represents, then the social uplift that King refers to will be prioritized above profit. Human dignity and interdependence, while it appears to have no economic profit, will be rewarded by thriving and surviving of the human race.

War is an outdated method for resolving conflict due to the genius nature of scientific advancement of this age. With so much imagination, creativity and inventiveness of the times, it would appear that humans would be able to imagine new ways settling disagreements without violence or war. With the invention of the internet and social media the cultures of the world have developed closer ties with greater awareness and understanding. The nations of the world are more interconnected than ever before. More of the same interests and concerns are shared than in previous ages and generations. Dr. Martin Luther King Jr. argues that such inventiveness should be redirected for peace, togetherness, and human flourishing. The struggle for domination and the competition for power is futile, but a comparable unified struggle for peace will have long lasting results.

> *Somehow, we must transform the dynamics of the world power struggle from the nuclear arms race, which no one can win, to a creative contest to harness man's genius for the purpose of making peace and prosperity a reality for all the nations of the world (Ibid, 182).*

Since the end of World War II, there have been fewer wars within European borders. NATO and the United Nations have created an environment and forum where diplomacy can flourish. Diplomatic organizations have developed around the world for the sake of peace and international cooperation. Certainly, the Vietnam War comes to mind, but the threat of war between the U.S. and Russia never came to be. Most of the wars today are not between nuclear powers but smaller ethnic or tribal skirmishes. Although there are fewer conflicts between global power, this is not enough. Although there are fewer civil wars, the temporary absence of violence should not cause one to rest satisfied. King suggests that the nations of the world should not be content when there is no violence. He declares that true nonviolence involves sustained, *persistent and determined efforts* for peace, harmony, and justice in the world (Ibid, 182). He further adds that the failure to prioritize diplomacy over the pursuit of war is not merely problematic but *a tragic death wish* (Ibid, 185). We cannot help but mention that the majority of the wars fought by the Western world in recent times have been acted out within nations inhabited by people of color. This is especially true of the global war on terror. Illegal invasions and drone strikes within those countries have been normalized. This has occurred within Somalia, Yemen, Syria, Libya, Iraq, Afghanistan, and Haiti. The military weakness of these countries is manipulated and abused to give permission of the US to act without consequence. They too are sovereign humanity and must be equally respected.

Beyond the need to prioritize peace, diplomacy and international cooperation is the need for a genuine love for humanity. To love humanity is to love self, for all are of the same blood under God and are connected in ways that cannot be fully appreciated. Utilizing modern-day inventiveness for the peaceful existence of humanity is important but insufficient; love for one another must be preeminent. Dr. King identified love as an absolute necessity for the survival of the human race. According to King, this is the foundational principle that *unites the great religions of the world belief* is that the force of love is the greatest power for good in the world (Ibid, 186). Love will drive away hate, greed, selfishness, and the evils of the world. Love will lead the world to not merely tolerate and respect the differences of the various cultures of the world but to embrace and value them. The Christological concept of the Christ death on the Cross demonstrates what love truly means. The Cross shows that love is willingness to lay down one's life for the salvation of others, rather than take life for the purpose of self-preservation or ambition.

The ushering in of a new world where violence is rejected, and war is no longer a method of achieving national or ethnic goals, is of urgent importance. It is not merely an idealistic dream but is an absolute imperative for the future of the human race. In a world where more nations are developing nuclear weapons, the likelihood of a nuclear holocaust becomes more possible. It becomes an even greater danger when there are nations who believe that they have a duty before the Sovereign of the universe to exact revenge upon their religious enemies. During the closing days of World War II, the United States attacked its wartime enemy, which was Japan. The American military responded in a disproportionately inhumane retaliatory assault. Two atomic bombs/nuclear bombs were dropped on the Japanese cities of Nagasaki and Hiroshima. Within seconds these two cities were disintegrated into smoldering ruins. It was a sudden and unexpected attack that destroyed hundreds of thousands of lives in an instant.

Today's nuclear technology far exceeds that of the late 1940s, which has the capacity to deliver a markedly superior amount of cataclysmic damage. In the 1940s there was only one nuclear power plant in the world. Today there are a significantly greater number of nations that have developed either nuclear weapons or other weapons of mass destruction. Today's nuclear technology has spread not only through Europe, but also China, India, and Pakistan, which hold some of the world's largest populations. Additionally, such technology is suspected to be possessed by many extremists' non-state actors. The use of drones to attack others is also becoming widespread and difficult to guard against. Even without nuclear weapons, weapons of mass destruction in the hands of extremist militant actors have the capacity to kill tens of thousands. Nuclear weapons are said to be deterrents and never intended for actual usage. Should they ever be launched, scores of the world's large cities may come under attack and be destroyed. In such a scenario, hundreds of millions of lives would be destroyed. Fears such as these are expressed in Dr. King's "Drum Major Instinct" sermon, which is referred to earlier in this thesis, *if somebody doesn't bring an end to this suicidal thrust that we see in the world today, none of us are going to be around, because somebody's going to make the mistake through our senseless blunderings of dropping a nuclear bomb somewhere (King, 1968).* Such a nuclear exchange can easily spiral out of control and spread throughout the globe. The world's infrastructure would be incapacitated which could possibly lead to a sustained *World War III* nuclear holocaust (Kagan, 2017). Mutual dialogue concerning the futility of nuclear weapons is desperately needed and absolute disarmament is a must. The continual development and study of nuclear weapons increases year by year, raising the possibility of such a holocaust. In the past wars were fought on a regional scale, but the post-modern world is much more connected through globalism and cyberspace. The wars that would potentially be fought in the future have more international implications than in the past. Societies are more connected and have greater reach. Making war an obsolete method must first begin with nuclear disarmament. Actions such as these require not only love for humanity but also faith in the goodness of humanity. Nation states which disarm, may be skeptical that others may fail to disarm, which makes them vulnerable to those who refuse. In this case, the Pauline characterization of love must be implemented which *thinks no evil* (1 Corinthians 13:5). Some nations must go first, and it should begin with the most powerful. To do so, nations must rediscover the value of life and the design of humanity by its Creator.

> *President John F. Kennedy said on one occasion, "[Humanity] must put an end to war or war will put an end to [humanity]." ...If we assume that life is worth living and that [humanity] has a right to survive, then we must find an alternative to war (King 1967: 180).*

Dr. King further argued that today's civilization is too advanced and prosperous to feel the need to compete for Earth's resources. Current society has such an extraordinary number of technological and scientific geniuses and, that it seems foolish to be fearful of scarcity and a lack of resources. He saw that war was more acceptable in the *past generations*, but this is no longer the case due to the advanced knowledge and capacity for discovery of the present times (Ibid, 178). King saw that without such a reordering of the world and introduction of such revolutionary values, *we shall destroy ourselves in the misuse of our own instruments* (Ibid, 171). In an age where it is understood that humans have the greatest capacity for self-destruction, nation states are enslaved by profitability of weapon making and aircraft carrier construction. The greatest prosperity, it must be understood, is the development of a world culture, where the survival and progress of the human family is the supreme profit.

6.5 Reconciliation is not merely personal piety, generous platitudes, and sentiments but political, social, and economic change.

Internationally recognized and respected theologian, John W. De Gruchy, shaped by the South African experience in the freedom struggle, distinguishes commonly held views on reconciliation and the realities of the gospel. Reconciliation means much more than a cessation of hatred and hostilities. De Gruchy brings to view that while reconciliation indeed demands and end of hatred, it cannot be separated from political and social endeavors and changes. He provides a holistic view of the gospel as it relates to revolutionary change combined with being reconciled with humanity from an interpersonal and relational standpoint. Additionally, De Gruchy argues that attempts to limit reconciliation to changes in sentiments amounts to a *theological travesty*.

> *It would be a theological travesty to give an account of the Christian doctrine of reconciliation in a way that confined it to the realm of personal piety and relations, or to the sphere of the Church (De Gruchy 2002: 1).*

Professor James Cone adds to De Gruchy's views that reconciliation is too often limited to the exercise of kindness, courtesy, and respect between populations without seeking to alleviate the painful histories that led to estrangement. Cone suggests that reconciliation requires revolutionary actions in destroying systems and structures that have created antipathy and societal division. The removal of societal orders that create disharmony can be considerably painful for those who have enjoyed the benefits and privileges of such systems, but genuine love would regard such pain as a small price to pay for the good of all. Additionally, Cone calls for those who have suffered the most within discriminatory system to accept their divine reconciliation by struggling against such systems that would deny them the privileges of divine acceptance. The gospel of reconciliation, according to Cone, involves eliminating systems that create divisions based on race or economic status. It destroys social systems which embrace social hierarchies which divide humanity into categories of slaves and masters. Howard Thurman made a profound statement connecting human dignity with equality and reconciliation. Thurman envisions a world where *advantage due to accident of birth or position is reduced to zero. Instead of relation between the weak and the strong there is merely a relationship between human beings...The awareness of this fact marks the supreme moment of human dignity* (Thurman 1976: 63). This is the essence of social reconciliation. The gospel demands that all are treated the same. It is not only the work of the powerful to dismantle such systems, but it is the work of the disempowered to aggressively stand against authority structures that separate humans into boxes of more worthy and less worthy. He distinguishes between true reconciliation and sentimental platitudes surrounding the idea of reconciliation. According to cone, the theology of reconciliation involves practical participation in socio-economic revolution, and that wherever such activity is seen, it must be understood to be the work of God. Metaphorical holding hands with former oppressors is insufficient.

> *There can be no communication between masters and slaves until the status of master no longer exists. [Reconciliation involves] destroying their pretensions to authority and ridiculing the symbols of power. It is not holding hands and singing "We shall overcome (Cone 1997: 344)."*

Theologians Duke Kwon and Gregory Thompson who focused on the importance of reparations where generational theft has occurred as important for reconciliation, argued for legitimate relational work as additional to the work of justice and repair. Kwon and Thompson agree that sentimental reconciliation is insufficient and that the work of justice is indispensable, but that there must be a sustained future endeavor to create genuine relationships between communities where none existed. This relational work goes beyond coexistence, but continued political, social and economic bridgebuilding. It goes beyond ending wars. North Korea and South Korea are not presently engaged in the exchange of military gunfire. There has been little bloodshed between the two Koreas since the Korean war, yet most diplomats would agree that it is less than ideal. The border between the Koreas is extremely militarized. This is an example of coexisting without the work of demilitarizing and developing community relationships. The Koreas manage to coexist, but suspicions remain. They are an example of what it looks like when political agreements are made and the work of relational bridgebuilding is neglected. This is not the model for the world and is not consistent with Christological reconciliation. It involves more than exchanges of ambassadors and diplomatic statecraft but envisioning a future together as genuine friends and siblings of the human family.

> *The Christian tradition calls this type of relational work reconciliation. However, reconciliation is not simply the cessation of hostilities or the willingness to coexist. It is, rather, about the cultivation of friendship and the creation of a community that bears witness to the reality of life beyond estrangement (Kwon and Thompson 2021: 43).*

Cone argues that there must be repentance and conversion rather than exchanges of sympathy on the part of the one who has been an oppressor. Such sympathies, Cone suggests, do not flow from a spirit of genuine reconciliation. Conversion is what is needed, which brings about a *radical reorientation of values (Cone 1997: 349)*, ethics and conduct, which involves forsaking the sinful structures and attitudes of racial or class superiority and the cultural dominance of those who have been treated inhumanely. Cone further adds that *to be reconciled with white people means fighting against their power to enslave, reducing masters to the human level, thereby making them accountable to black liberation* (Cone 1997: 345).

Cone understood that there must be a new birth of faith that will lead former oppressors to join the struggle in dismantling systems that distinguish population groups in ways that that dehumanize.

Although it is welcomed, it is not enough to renounce personal prejudice, but to counteract the diabolical work of enslavement, exploitation, and exclusion.

> *The law of love has required Christians not simply to repent of their personal prejudices but also to labor toward relational reconciliation—to live lives not of exclusion but of embrace...And yet we are conscious that this way of seeing American racism, as a relational division that demands the work of racial reconciliation, is incomplete (Kwon and Thompson 2021: 44).*

While many in the American evangelical church today do not see racism as a problem, or turn a blind eye to it, there are those who stand apart. One widely respected White evangelical pastor, Robert Morris preached a highly touted sermon on racial reconciliation and the gospel. It must be noted that pastor Morris pastors a 36,000-member congregation called Gateway Church. He has been a leading voice on reconciliation. He suggests that tearing down the walls of ignorance will bridge social gaps and lead to reconciliation.

> *We'll never understand until we walk around the other side, what some people that you work with, that live in your neighborhood, that come to our church. What they and their families have been through. And it's time for the church to stand up and declare that racism is evil, and the answer is Jesus Christ... Our nation needs a healing. We keep looking to Washington to solve it; they're not going to solve it. The church is going to solve this problem (Morris 2017: Sermon).*

More voices such as Morris are needed if true reconciliation is to occur. Perhaps voices such as Morris will unshackle other clergypersons, who have been shy concerning this topic, will begin to speak out.

The reconciliation that the cross of Jesus impacts is much more than spiritual expressions and commitments to cease from hatred. No reconciliation as it relates to human relations can be considered legitimate, which excludes the political and economic liberation aspects. When the cries of the hurting and broken population groups on planet earth are not heeded and remain unaddressed, the ministry of reconciliation remains unfulfilled. Christian theologians who live in the world's most powerful nations, often see nothing but greatness and humanitarianism within their nations and their allies. They fail to understand the damage, division and chaos which is caused by those nations where they originate. Christian theologians, in order to engage in the work of reconciliation, must cease self-justification and defensiveness of the histories of the great nations of the world. Unconditional commitment to the state of Israel and defending the history of colonialism needs to be replaced with an undeniable and sustained commitment to political and social liberation for the sake of the work of reconciliation. Those who struggle for the liberation that divine reconciliation demands must not be discouraged by the blindness of the most privileged classes but must continue with faith that a brighter day is coming. There is no other choice. Moreover, according to Cone, the problem with Western Christian theology, is its tendency that divine reconciliation is non-political, non-tangible, non-practical but merely spiritual. To achieve reconciliation is to correct the spiritualized views of it, which are embraced by so many. Cone states the following concerning the theology of reconciliation and its practical aspects in restoring the oppressed to their God-given rights and privileges.

> *And it is likely that they will continue to rationalize the meaning of divine reconciliation in "spiritual" and nonpolitical terms. But God's will to liberate the little ones and to bring them "home to glory" will not be defeated by white piety or rhetoric. The new age is coming in, and through God's will to reconcile the oppressed to God (Cone 1997: 343).*

Understanding Christian reconciliation as more than a spiritual experience between the individual and God, and between the individual and their neighbor, is a must. Reconciliation has a political and socio-economic dimension also, which cannot be ignored. Jemar Tisby encapsulates the wrongheaded views of too many in the American Evangelical Church. He expostulates how Evangelical views of reconciliation are too narrow, too spiritualized and too individualistic. He addresses many of the mistakes American Evangelicals make in their attempts to implement the reconciliation that Jesus demanded. One area Tisby challenges White Christians is how they often view racism as merely isolated incidents of personal prejudice, rather than political activities and national policies. Consequently, their answer to reconciliation, is to include more races in their church services and in their ecclesiastical positions.

> *In this understanding, the forces that separate people of different races and ethnicities come from personal prejudice. An individualistic understanding of reconciliation presents racial separation as the problem.... When evangelicals focus on bringing people together, they often leave out any analysis of the systemic and institutional forces that led to the separation in the first place. Occasional racial proximity is too low a goal for reconciliation (Tisby 2021: 81).*

Oftentimes whites in America believe that reconciliation is being accomplished if they are not expressing hatred and blacks are in close proximity to them. They fail to realize that it is possible to love the black neighbor or co-worker who does not in their view fit the stereotype, and not deeply love and appreciate the black population and its culture. Tisby is correct that this too low a goal and falls short of Jesus' vision. In order to achieve reconciliation, white people must be able to imagine a world where they are not the center. In other words, reconciliation does not merely involve white's including black people in their spaces but involves understanding that those spaces do not belong to them. They must recognize that they are one of many cultures, who have rights to the same space and must learn how they may contribute within a multicultural framework. This concept demands that they learn from others from a position of humility. Reconciliation in the American context is not achieved by placing black people in positions of power, where they become new drivers of unjust systems. It means demolishing those systems and erecting righteous and just systems. Tisby further suggests that reconciliation also means celebrating other cultures without the expectation of assimilation or leaving their cultures or people behind in order to be included.

> *Racial reconciliation must also address how power is mediated through culture...What evangelical racial reconciliation often means for Black people and other people of color is leaving their own communities to join predominantly white churches... and learning under mainly white leadership. This is not integration; it is assimilation (Ibid., 81).*

From an eschatological point of view, the day will come when full reconciliation for the historically excluded will occur. It is the work of Christ's followers to introduce and struggle for the values of the new age in this present reality. To neglect such a work adds to the pain of exclusion and marginalization in this present age. It is the work of Christian discipleship to remove barriers to equality as the day of the new age hastens onward. In this case hope remains despite the attitudes of those who misrepresent and fail to appreciate the genuine work of reconciliation.

6.6 Nations and population groups must view themselves as one reconciled human race of global citizens.

The cataclysmic effects of climate change, nuclear proliferation, epidemics, and poverty threaten all humans everywhere. These are common enemies of humanity. To defeat them requires united action by all nations, races, and ethnicities. Much of the competition, unresolvable hostilities, and legitimate disputes among nations and ethnic groups seem small when compared to the threats to human survival which exist in the world. The severity of these challenging issues helps human beings to realize their common vulnerabilities and their undeniable interdependence on each other for survival and progress. The issues surrounding justice and repair become more critical because they pave the way for ethnic and international harmony. It is this harmony that is needed to address the threats of today. Exploitation, market manipulation, unending wars and displacement undermines the international familyhood that is needed to address the larger and more ominous threats to human flourishing.

> *The problems we face are global, and the solutions can only be found as we tackle them together as citizens of a world threatened by alienation, enmity and violence. Whatever the role of nation states today, or the importance of contexts for understanding and dealing with issues, borders and boundaries cannot and should not be allowed to insulate people or universal concerns for justice and peace (De Gruchy 2002: 11).*

Dr. Martin Luther King argues that humanity oftentimes fails to recognize how much each nation and race has historically contributed to an advanced society. All have been dependent on the wisdom, inventiveness and perspectives of other races and ethnicities. When this interdependence is analyzed, it will be seen how interconnected the human family has always been. This reality of interdependence is not only seen in the past but fails to be appreciated in the present. King argues that we are already connected, "whether we realize it or not." He further adds that because of the contributions that each society makes, benefiting the whole, that all are truly indebted to one another. *Whether we realize it or not, each of us lives eternally "in the red." We are everlasting debtors to known and unknown men and women* (King 1967: 178). The global citizenry would not be the same and would lose a little of itself without the contribution of all. Therefore, when others are hurting, and are unable to live out their full potential, they all unknowingly feel the pain. What King expresses regarding interdependence is like an African concept called Ubuntu or what some theologians refer to as Ubuntu theology. Professor Michael Battle an episcopal priest and theologian, who is a scholar in the area of Ubuntu theology and the life and works of Archbishop Desmond Tutu. Professor Battle connects the philosophy of Ubuntu with the Christian message. Battle refers to the "out-of-sync cosmology that many Western Christians have for God's communal nature." He describes God's view of Ubuntu in contrast with the individualistic focus of Western theology and practice in the following language:

In an individualistic world, there is too much noise and too many distractions prohibiting the hearer to reckon with what is the essential message of Christianity. Trapped in ourselves, there is little incentive to strive for the joy beyond self. With community, however, the noise of otherness can become a symphony orchestra in which each particular part knows its uniqueness in relationship to each other. This is Ubuntu, and this can become heaven on earth (Battle 2017: 46).

Western Christians quite often pride themselves in the material successes of the capitalistic worlds in which they live, without regard to how financially exploitative and predatory their economies may be. A survival of the fittest society does not square with the godly view of interdependence that allows us to see ourselves in each other. African American Theologian, and graduate of Midwestern Seminary, Claude Atcho, writes in his book, *Reading Black Books,* about a *communal hope that emerges from a communal identity that senses and finds that one's own fate and wellbeing are tied up in that of another. It is a belief that includes and transcends an individual and is practiced by the individual for the whole* (Atcho 2022: 166). In order to achieve reconciliation, whatever stands in the way of human flourishing, particularly the historically marginalized and exploited, the concept of Ubuntu must be emphasized and embraced. It is true that personal responsibility or private morality is vital, and personal success should be celebrated, but these principles should be understood in the context of interdependence, reconciled togetherness and equality. Battle contrasted the Western Christian philosophy which centers self and privatization with the concept of Ubuntu which centers interdependence, community and neighborhood. He explains that Ubuntu and the tenet of "Love thy neighbor as thyself" are one and the same. Westerners, due to their strong emphasis on individualism, and fear of depending on others, may misunderstand Ubuntu. Westerners may have difficulty realized that self is developed and understands its purpose in relationship to community. We all need each other whether we realize it or not. This is one of the barriers to the reconciliation that Jesus envisioned.

> *In a Western worldview, interdependence may be easily confused with codependence, a pathological condition in which people share a dependence on something that is not life-giving, such as alcohol or drugs. Ubuntu, however, is about symbiotic and cooperative relationships—neither the parasitic and destructive relationships of codependence nor the draining and alienating relationships of competition (Battle 2009: 12).*

This culture of reconciled togetherness and global citizenry it is not simply a good idea for the future, but it is necessary in order to fight and to meet the challenges other 21st century which includes issues that threaten human survival such as: fighting against pandemics, epidemics, climate change, unclean drinking water, deforestation, dismantling nuclear weapons, and fighting infectious diseases such as HIV and social conditions such poverty. The COVID 19 pandemic has put on display how vulnerable human beings are on the planet and how the COVID-19 pandemic did not respect national or hemispheric boundaries. The COVID-19 virus attacked human beings wherever they were as one and a same. It did not have any regard for race, national origin, economic standing or ethnic differences. We have seen in the COVID-19 pandemic how important international cooperation and human togetherness was necessary simply from a logistical point of view. It showed how intricately linked human societies have always been. As of this writing, five-million people have died because of the COVID pandemic; this is true despite the advanced logistical and scientific technology that exists. Could it be that if there was more international cooperation and dialogue that millions of lives might have been saved? What does this suggest about future pandemics? Will bridges of communication and global interaction improve that will assist in the next pandemic? Dr. King's words concerning the interconnectedness of the human race cannot be more clearly seen than in the COVID 19 pandemic. It is clear as King states, that *We are all involved in the single process.*

Whatever affects one directly affects all indirectly. We are all links in the great chain of humanity (King 2013: 26). Dr. King's concept of persons and societies being "links in the great chain of humanity" is also Ubuntu philosophy. This view was later advanced by Archbishop Desmond Tutu. Professor Michael Battle cites Archbishop Tutu to explain how Ubuntu is to be viewed and lived out on the world, and how it reflects Christ's demands for reconciliation.

> *'A person with Ubuntu is open and available to others, affirming of others, does not feel threatened that others are able and good, for he or she has a proper self-assurance that comes from knowing that he or she has a proper self-assurance that comes from knowing that he or she belongs in a greater whole and is diminished when others are humiliated and diminished, when others are tortured and oppressed (Battle 2009: 14).*

The fact that all nations, races, backgrounds, and economic classes are divinely connected and considered to be as one, may be viewed as such through the Christian sacraments. Catholicism's holiest sacrament (along with other historic traditions) is often viewed as the celebration of the Eucharist during mass. The entire community, rich or poor, kings or paupers, all drink from the same cup and eat from the same bread. This is a prime example of how fellow humans should view themselves as partakers of God's creation, no one should be excluded based on ethnicity or tribe. The creation is God's gift to humans, and all are obligated to share from the perspective of community and common good.

> *In the church all classes and races drink from the one cup and eat the one bread, and so share equally in the good that gathers the church...Unless a community is fallen so deeply that its common good is in fact a poison, a chief goal of its political striving must always be equal sharing of that good (Soulen and Woodhead 2006: 45).*

In the same way that African revolutions began and succeeded when tribalism was set aside for a larger African identity (Mandela, 1994,) the same way the following the Rwandan genocide, Rwandans set aside tribalism and educated themselves to view themselves as Rwandans first, then it is possible on a global scale as humans. This does not mean that the less powerful should assimilate into the larger or dominant culture and set aside its distinct features. It does mean that tribe or culture should not seek its own progress at the expense of others, but in harmony with others. All cultures reflect the creativity of the divine and have developed within themselves much that can contribute the whole of humanity. Pan-Africanism also reflects the ideal that the whole is stronger in combating common challenges together rather than standing apart in separate compartments of tribe and ethnic groups. Many fear that by coming together beyond tribe or race may cause one to lose the distinctive historical features, but it is possible through deliberate action to preserve the best qualities of each. It is the diverse nature and contributions of tribes that should be embraced and supported rather than tribalism itself. Strength is found not only in togetherness but the distinctive qualities which each brings to the table. It is possible to love and connect to ethnic neighbors and embrace the diversity of each. One should not require others to change and mirror one another's cultural identities in order to demonstrate love and work for reconciliation. Dr. King argues that loyalty to the whole of the human race works to preserve the unique greatness of all tribes, races, nations, and societies rather than detract.

> *Every nation must now develop an overriding loyalty to [humankind] as a whole in order to preserve the best in their individual societies. This call for a worldwide fellowship that lifts neighborly concern beyond one's tribe, race, class and nation is in reality a call for an all-embracing and unconditional love for all [humans] (King 1967: 186).*

Archbishop Desmond Tutu is legendary in this regard and was a powerful voice during the South African freedom struggle against apartheid. Following the fall of the white supremacist apartheid regime in 1994 in South Africa, there was an urgent need for the nation to address its history of injustices in order to move forward together in the future. The Truth and Reconciliation Commission (also known by the abbreviation TRC) was formed where honest dialogue could occur between blacks, whites and other population groups concerned about the past. Desmond Tutu was the highest profile clergyman in South Africa at the time and used his words and works to bring about reconciliation and healing in a country that had been traumatized by the history of brutal white supremacy. The TRC became a forum where South Africans of various racial categories could understand the fears, hopes and desires of all people within the country. According to Tutu, much knowledge was obtained concerning various groups which were forcefully separated by skin color since 1948. Those who participated in the TRC, and observed the proceedings, discovered that they all had more in common than they had differences. The TRC is a model of what can be accomplished when citizens of the world genuinely open the door to dialogue and discovery. Though there were different skin colors, people who were oppressed by the old regime, and those who benefitted from it, they learned that they all shared the same human desire for life and liberty. Those who were afraid of retaliation by blacks learned that their fears were unfounded. Tutu described the commission as having made a *scientific discovery* in this way.

> *They discovered not a Colored, a black, an Indian, a white. No, they found fellow human beings. What a profound scientific discovery that blacks, Coloreds (usually people of mixed race), and Indians were in fact human beings, who had the same concerns and anxieties and aspirations...and almost none wanted to drive the whites into the sea. They just wanted their place in the sun (Tutu 1999: 8).*

The United Nations is a helpful diplomatic forum where fellow nations can come together and discuss areas of disagreement and commonality, but it is insufficient in the work of addressing past injustices and working together for freedom. Many of its findings and contributions have been helpful when analyzing problematic situations within nations around the world. It cannot be compared to the TRC in this way. The TRC is more targeted at situations within nations, whereas the United Nations is committed to diplomacy. The problem with the United Nations is that the nations who are most economically and militarily powerful are rarely held accountable for their violations of international law, particularly in the case of Middle Eastern conflicts and the Israeli occupation of Palestinian territory. These powerful nations have the votes within the UN security council and can hold up decisions and provide political shelter for their allies. The United Nations is helpful in many ways but is politically incapable of bringing about justice and reconciliation. However, Truth and Reconciliation needs to occur within nations between tribes and ethnic groups and between colonial powers and former colonies. It must occur between Western nations and those who have been historically exploited by them, and between corporations and workers who have been denied just wages. Inherent in the name "Truth and Reconciliation" is the call for truth. Reconciliation cannot occur without truth, righteousness and justice. Truth is oftentimes more difficult than reconciliation, but as seen in the case of South Africa, it is certainly achievable. The TRC was not perfect but nonetheless effective and provides a foundation that can easily be improved upon by those who follow its lead.

6.7 An economy of grace is needed in order encourage global familyhood and avoid future conflicts.

Predatory economic systems must be replaced with a global economy of grace. Christian communities from the west must educate themselves out of the view that exploitative capitalism and neo-colonial systems are inherently Christian, because white Christians developed them. An economy based on justice and mutual respect is urgently needed. Because Western societies embrace predatory capitalism as well as Christian ethics, many assume that such an economic system is fair and just. History shows that this is far from the truth. In fact, it undermines the New Testament command *"Thou shalt not muzzle the ox while he is threshing and the labourer is worthy of his wages* (1 Timothy 5:18 NASB.) The predatory capitalistic system of today's economy fails to place the highest value on human dignity and labor but places the greatest value on profit and the maximum enrichment of a few. The New Testament in the above statement encourages the powerful to give special attention to the sacred dignity and divine regard for those who plow the fields. Today this would apply to the poor and low wage earners in the world who are victims of the global market system. One highly regarded theologian, Dwight Hopkins, who is a Harvard University graduate and professor of Black Christian theology speaks to this issue. Dwight Hopkins offers an important perspective about human dignity and the management of Earth's resources in a particularly profound statement in his writings. Hopkins offered the following analysis by connecting black American theology and the global movement to reconcile the world economic powers and those who have historically suffered from its greed. His argument shows why reconciliation must include removing the barriers to global economic justice and casting out the demons of economic slavery and dependency through the political activity of the church. Hopkins refers to the good news of being Black and Christian throughout the world, and how black people are celebrating liberation as the foundation of the gospel story. Hopkins believes that this phenomenon has a direct connection to the global freedom struggle for the exploited and dehumanized. Hopkins further states that wherever people in the world majority (darker races) are free, this provides a paradigm of hope for others. Hopkins adds:

> *If the majority of the people in the world who are materially and spiritually oppressed are also free, then this offers hope to remove the unjust power of the minority groups which control most of the world's resources. Removing the internal and external 'demons' keeping the world's population in slavery will help change the structural system of global monopolization by a few (Hopkins 1999: 12).*

Hopkins' analysis is in line with the New Testament concept of economic justice and reconciliation. The New Testament suggests that the worker should not be denied an equitable share of the work that is performed. Additionally, the Virgin Mary sang a divinely inspired eschatological song which brought to view the reordering of world structures under the reign of the Messiah. One significant verse in that song stated, *He hath filled the hungry with good things; and the rich he hath sent empty away* (Luke 1:53 KJV.)

Some may suggest that such a statement by Mary must be limited by spiritual realities, but what is true in the spiritual world is also valid in the natural world. It is true that those who feel that they are spiritually rich and do not need a teacher will go away not being filled with Christ's gospel, while those who hunger after God will be filled. It is also true that those who are physically hungry, its Christ's objective to fill them, while those who value material wealth over human dignity will lose their own humanity in the process, and the blessings which were offered. The global market system has little concern with feeding the hungry with good things but sending them away empty.

> *The global market system endangers human dignity by putting all localities and communities in jeopardy and thus preventing for great numbers of people the communal belonging necessary to human dignity. For millions of people globalization has not meant the enhancement of life; it does not work for most of the world's abject poor and working poor...they have felt in increasingly subject to forces beyond their control (Soulen and Woodhead 2006: 173).*

The valuing of human dignity demanded by Christian anthropology forbids the exploitation of labor for the enrichment of a few. Valuing human dignity in a world economy demands that workers should never go hungry, be able to provide decent housing for themselves and their families, the ability to clothe themselves and their families, and to occupy their own land. There is enough wealth in the world where corporations can employ workers that can live in dignity and happiness and for the job creators to remain wealthy. Workers who are not valued and barely survive in the economy are not truly poor; they are rich in skills and abilities, yet these riches are stolen through starvation wages. Moreover, in many cases the global market system pollutes and depletes the environment and deprives its workers, which is also a denial of dignity.

One of the most minerally rich areas of the world, of which all the technologically advanced nations of the world are indebted is the Democratic Republic of Congo. This country is a perfect prototype of how the minerally rich are exploited and dehumanized in the global marketplace. Coltan, an ore found in Congo, is indispensable for the creation of electronic devices of which virtually all societies are dependent. Mobile phones, lap tops, smart TVs, printers, remotes and other unmentioned items that are commonly utilized in the world are products of coltan. Most observers of world affairs are aware of the conflicts among the militias which occupy eastern Congo, which plays a major role in the extraction of minerals in the region. The Rwandan and Ugandan government work through proxy militias in the struggle for Congo's resources. According to James H. Smith, professor of anthropology at the University of California, Davis, who has written exhaustively about the eastern Congo, says that it must be understood that the conflicts between the militias do not originate with the struggle for mineral wealth, and would indeed exist without it.

The original sin which created the fighting among the various factions began with the dehumanizing campaign to partition Africa along political lines for the economic benefit and power sharing among the Europeans. The fighting in eastern Congo is a multi-generational symptom of the original sin. According to Smith, because of all of the mineral wealth in eastern Congo, there is little incentive for Europeans or Americans to correct the historical wrongs and help end the fighting, which helps outside parties in their economic ambitions. The question must be asked, "Who supplies the weapons for the fighting in eastern Congo in this country with 90 million people who speak 250 different languages?" Another question might be as follows: "Why is the DRC, which is close to the size of Western Europe, and perhaps the most minerally wealthy, not an economic powerhouse in the world?" Smith suggests that the present-day conditions are rooted in the history stemming from 1885 and King Leopold, who conquered and colonized the area. Professor Smith tells his readers that this newly colonized area, now known as DRC, was then called "Congo Free State." Leopold viewed this territory as his privately owned real estate investment. This "real estate" venture functioned through violent extraction and murder. Much of the disputes over land by the inhabitants of Congo are the legacy of boundaries and borders created by ignorant Europeans, who had little reverence for Congolese humanity, but also close to zero understanding of the people who lived there. The Europeans saw value in the resources and only viewed the Congelese as things to be utilized in the extraction of raw materials. New discoveries of previously unknown materials continue to emerge on a regular basis in the Congo. Smith further expounds upon the natural wealth of the region and the capitalist hunger among the "advanced societies" for what Congo possesses.

> *The territory, which contains one of the largest forests in the world, turned out to also be one of the most resource-rich places in the world; to this day, new raw materials spring forth from Congo seemingly like magic, to feed each new 'stage' of capitalist growth and empire building...* (Smith 2022: 20.)

According to professor Smith, in what was known as the Belgian Congo, there was the pretense of humanitarianism by developing the infrastructure of Congo, while simultaneously "exploiting and excluding" the miners of the area. It would be later discovered that the humanitarian infrastructure development was not necessarily for the purpose of aiding the Congolese, but for the purpose of moving raw materials to their intended destination (Ibid, 21).

Professor Smith further adds that during the Congolese wars, five million people died. He suggested that the wars were based on generational suffering resulting from the colonial past, yet these events occurred in the same time and space as the *"post-1980s 'digital revolution' and the global demand for minerals used in digital devises, almost all of which are found in great supply in the eastern Congo."* Smith also explains to his readers, who may understand the fighting as strictly related to the discovery of minerals, the complexities of the region. The explanation was especially needed for those who dismiss the Congolese crisis as another example of how violent people exist, without understanding the structures that create the violence.

As many scholars pointed out, the global demand for

> *minerals didn't cause the war, but it did finance combatants and incentivize neighboring countries and international corporate players to get involved in the trade and remain in the war...Though these wars were not caused by the demand for minerals and were to a great extent driven by localized conflicts over access to land rooted in colonial appropriations and resettlements, they cannot be fully understood without taking into account global events and processes (Ibid, 26).*

So, according to professor Smith, the fighting among militias in eastern Congo does not occur because the people of the region are instinctively violent, but because they are the victims of colonial violence, politics and empire building, and are simply struggling beneath the weight of that history. The historic wrongs from which they suffer makes the Congolese vulnerable to outside powers who desire to take advantage of them for their own gain. It is this vulnerable state that forms the greatest obstacle to Congolese self-determination and equally enjoying the fruits of its mineral wealth as well as their labor. American evangelicals must come to recognize that what they view as being a "blessed" nation from a material standpoint stems to a certain extent from the hardships and historical violence suffered by the Congolese. When this is realized, what is often viewed as "blessings" for supporting Israel's militarism, are in actuality the perks of empire building which dismisses the sacred humanity of the Congolese. An economy of grace would not count such as "blessings" while the Congolese do not fully benefit from their mineral wealth and labor, but will work to overturn economic systems and structures, and work to correct historical wrongs that stand in the way. Award winning investigator and author Christopher Vogel, points out how white saviorism unintentionally creates further hardships and complications for the Congolese, because it assumes to have all the answers for African conflicts, but fails to listen to those on the street level for advice on what remedies are needed. White saviorism, as Vogel explains, takes on an air of superiority where it feels that it is its role to rescue non-whites and marginalized communities by educating, advising, dictating and creating solutions for the problems that exist, without fully understanding or viewing them as equals. Those who are infected with white saviorism tend to view themselves (metaphorically speaking) as parent-like and those they seek to rescue as child-like. The commonly recognized paintings of a blonde-haired, white Jesus, seems to have some level of connection to this psychological phenomenon. According to Vogel, this complex often fails to examine the historical roots of conflict based on colonial structures. This concept of white saviorism seeks to simply the problems in the DRC and incorrectly views their complexities through the lens of Black villains and Black victims. In Christian theology, the Cross teaches that all persons need saving, both rich and poor. In this case, "white saviors" need to be saved from their own arrogance and tone deafness, while those whom they seek to save are in need of being saved from the consequences of said arrogance and tone deafness. This mindset is often witnessed by evangelical missionaries from the Western world who kindly engage in humanitarian service without realizing that those whom they aid also intelligent and may also serve and educate them in many areas.

> *The choice to foreground a story of Black villains and Black victims to justify tackling an economy seen as illegal and criminal—rather than advocating for structural changes in fighting the violence and inequality affecting Black lives in global supply chains—opened the doors for the mismatch between the stated aims of the 'conflict minerals' campaign and its outcomes (Vogel 2021: 24).*

One way in which further hardships were created through white saviorism was by creating a regulatory system in the Congo, by which high-tech companies could deal with local miners. These regulations had great intentions, under an American law named Dodd-Frank, but were based in ignorance. It was designed to reduce bloodshed, but generated more poverty and suffering. In some cases, mines were closed for various periods.

> *Faced with pressure from NGOs and civil society to reopen Congolese mining and buy Congolese minerals, high-tech companies such as Apple, Intel, and HP, operating in the*

context of Dodd-Frank, needed to ensure that the smelters from which they bought processed ore were doing so from blood-free sites through a reliable conflict free or blood free system (Smith 2022: 37).

In order to achieve an economy of grace, those who would be white saviors, must take a posture of humility, and possess a willingness to educated themselves out of their ignorance and become more acquainted with the history of the region and the political dynamics. Those who live in countries which enjoy the luxuries which result from the mineral wealth of the Congo, should not assume that the Congolese do not have the answer to resolve their conflicts. They should also deprogram themselves from the stereotypes which they have concerning this region. Another example of white saviorism as boycotting smartphones, smart tv devices, and tablets in order to protest the violence against women in the mining sectors. Others may suggest sanctions or more trade regulations. Yet this misunderstands the issues about the wars and the demands of the mining workforce. Vogel corrects many wrong assumptions about the area, and why it is important to allow the Congolese to be the educators in this matter:

> *However, while the quick fix would be to refuse to buy every other new smartphone on the market, it would not really have an impact...[because] rape is not causally related to mining (it does, however, correlate with war and social breakdown, amongst other phenomena). A Congolese petty trader, in turn, might deplore how war has eroded non-mining livelihoods, and that violent exploitation of minerals has contributed to entrenching a climate of impunity. She might also add that the preponderance of mining in eastern Congo's economy has unmade the equilibrium of agriculture, cattle-herding, timber, craft and trade, replacing subsistence with dependence (Vogel 2021: 25).*

This understanding of the devastation of the cattle herding and agricultural sectors due to over two-hundred years of extraction and its impact on the Congolese ecosystem might explain why this minerally wealthy country is not among the actual wealthy. The continued destabilization due to the politics and empire building of colonial times presents a major barrier for the Congolese to become as prosperous as those who benefit from their mineral wealth. The economic incentives to ignore the current destabilization is real. Who will examine and overturn the systems as Jesus overturned the moneychangers' tables in Jerusalem? Faith understands that there is enough prosperity in the world for all to survive and live out their purpose and enjoy fruitfulness. Such activity would be good news to the poor in the DRC because it may serve to *invert the assumed hierarchy of the world order and bring the world to Congo, such that Congo suddenly becomes a center that sets the pace for the rest of the world, rather than an alleged 'dark corner' that lagged behind or defied civilization or modernity* (Smith 2022: 34). This is the turning upside down of the social order that the early apostles of Jesus referenced (Acts 17:6).

Catholic theologian Josee' Ngalula, who is Congolese, lectures in several theological institutes on the continent. She is a noted theology professor at the Catholic University of Congo and also at the Al Mowafaqa Ecumenical Institute in Rabat, Morocco. In reference to the violence of her homeland, she states that *"The reality of violence is at the heart of the message of Christianity, which celebrates Good Friday and places Jesus Christ, the victim of violence, at the heart of the faith...One cannot do theology without seeing Christ who challenges us in situations of suffering."* (Sarr, 2021).

It is important for Christian leaders in America, to see the violence in the Congo from a historical perspective. Christ has suffered violence at the hands of European powers through the bloodshed that has been inflicted upon the Congolese through their history, and by ignoring the structures that create and benefit from the bloodshed. Despite the doom and gloom of Congolese suffering, because of the technology that results from their labor, more people are aware of their plight. The devices that are the foundation of the information age, brings hope that a resurrection is on the horizon. In the same land where bloodshed and death were commonplace, the very substance that was used to exploit them, may be the means of their rising from their socio-economic grave. International communication and global awareness are increasing by the day. Amazingly, these same devices which require coltan, have also helped film the police brutality inflicted upon their black brothers and sisters in the U.S. Although a resurrection in the Congo is within view, the stone, as was in the case of Jesus, must be rolled away. Rolling the stone away means removing the historical barriers that have hindered the Congolese from emerging victorious.

In order for reconciliation to occur, American evangelicals must not view these indispensable devices and technological advancements simply as material "blessings," for being a land of "free market" faith and freedom, but as reminders of the structures which benefit their society and that tend to shackle and disenfranchise the most vulnerable populations of the world. Rather than claiming to represent a Jesus, (who is philosophically Eurocentric in the Evangelical imagination) who offers nationalistic "blessings" due to one's Anglo-Saxon "Christian" heritage, one should seek to embrace a Jesus who places premium value on victimized bodies and broken spirits above (the God bless the USA) material blessings. Author and theologian, Claude Atcho outlines the problematic nature of the Jesus of the Eurocentric and Evangelical imagination, who points the non-European to heaven, while failing to make prominent the Jesus whose heart was engaged in the earthly and material concerns (not merely in a humanitarian sense as Evangelicals emphasize but also in a systemic sense) of the exploited. He addresses the historic motivation behind such a misguided focus:

> *This Jesus, white in color and in concern, was a strictly transcendent Jesus, selectively concerned with the things above, heaven and eternity, so that white Christians might powerfully control the things below: profits, bodies and nations...We find that this Jesus is not simply transcendent but immanent, concerned not simply with heaven but with earth. Jesus is not a heavenly bystander to our suffering...He is the one who is 'near to the brokenhearted and who saves the crushed in spirit (Atcho 2022: 69).'*

The riches that grow out of predatory capitalism depend on the poverty of the workers which are employed. Predatory and plantation economies are counterproductive to the Christian work of reconciliation. Christian theology should address the unethical and dehumanizing aspects of such an economy. Dr. Martin Luther King Jr. addressed this issue. He suggested that it is the denial of dignity within the world's great economy that leads to conflicts, coups, and political violence. One cannot continue to lock others out of the blessings of the earthly kingdom, and not suffer the consequences of those desiring to break out of their unsustainable conditions.

> *One cannot hope to keep people locked out of the earthly kingdom of wealth, health and happiness. Either they share in the blessings of the world or they organize to break down and overthrow those structures or governments which stand in the way of their goals (King 1967: 173).*

One such action to overthrow such structures was the Cuban Revolution of 1954, which would subsequently lead to the US embargo upon Cuba. America's response to the Cuban Revolution and the Cuban Missile Crisis would eventually shut Cuba out from its economic potential. An economy of grace which brings reconciliation also means ending the 60-year Cuban economic embargo imposed by the United States military in 1962 at the beginning of the Cold War. Theologian and professor Ary Fernandez-Alban of the Presbyterian Reformed Church of Cuba, argues for the legitimacy of the Cuban Revolution based on Christian theology. Fernandez-Alban characterizes the revolution as a liberating and salvific program which also "unmasks the idolatrous character of Capitalism (Fernandez-Alban 2018: 9). He suggests that such a theology should not be a subject for which they should repent in order to appease the American government. The embargo upon Cuba is maintained based upon a political realignment which occurred during the Cuban Revolution and subsequent missile crisis (Ibid., 1). Today, it only serves to economically cripple and punish a tiny island which refuses to bow to the political interests of the American empire (Ibid, 3). Millions have unjustly suffered poverty, hardship and hunger due to a 60-

year-old dispute. The Soviet Union no longer exists, yet the economic punishment to this Island continues due to old hatreds. The American political system holds this posture because to do otherwise would bow to communism and admit that they have failed in their attempts to economically strong-arm the island nation (ibid ,21). To the U.S. this would be a sign of weakness. However, this is a paradoxical for a Christian right-wing political movement in America which adheres to a theology of forgiveness and second chances. Such a sinfully proud posture is the exact opposite of a Jesus, whom the right wing professes to worship, who humbled himself to identify with the suffering of humans, including his enemies, which he loved. The cross showed that humility is not a sign of weakness but the prerequisite for greatness. Most Cubans were not born during the time of the missile crisis, and are not responsible for the political fights of the past.

The right wing of the US political system hates being held accountable for its racist and xenophobic past, and desires to be forgiven, yet fails to forgive a 60-year grievance. "Why should we be held economically responsible for the sins of our forefathers" is a common refrain by the right wing of the US, but they do not extend the same economic grace to the Cuban population. To state that the embargo must remain due to human rights violations on the part of the Cuban government is hypocritical for a nation which unwaveringly supports the state of Israel's violations. Israel continues to violate international laws which are protecting human rights, because the US refuses to allow them to be held accountable before the United Nations. Additionally, the US lacks moral credibility to challenge Cuba on human rights, while its own government has been condemned by the United Nations in 2014 for its violations surrounding racial bias in policing and police brutality against black people (Moore 2014). The US should be as gracious to the Cuban family as much as it desires the world to be gracious unto themselves.

The justice of God, grace and reconciliation demands that the

US will no longer utilize its great power to lock the Cuban people out from full participation in the world economy. It is better to allow children to enjoy the fullness of their potential and the benefits of prosperity than to hold historical grudges. Ending the embargo would be good news for the poor, hungry and destitute on the Island. Such an action would not only benefit Cuban families, but the human family benefits. This is true because they will be enabled to maximize their potential and make their full contribution to the world society. Christian leaders, rather than seeking punish the Cubans economically, should be foremost in seeking reconciliation without demanding political submission and uniformity. The cross of Jesus means that the Cuban families living on the island are loved just as much by God's son as American families. Reconciliation means that rather than seeking to keep the Cubans crippled, those influential Christian leaders ought to use their proximity to power to heal them and help them walk again. The cross means that we are one humanity and should equally enjoy the blessings of Earth's resources and the fruit of one's potential.

Moving toward reconciliation and making the world a better place for the entire human race calls for an economic system that views the human not to an end which is designed to live in poverty so that a few will acquire billions. An economic system is needed where human beings will be appreciated and respected as created for the praise of glorification of the divine. Justice demands that even those who labor in the so-called low skilled jobs will also share in the blessings of prosperity; Christian anthropology demands that all will be able to live in dignity. Human beings, which are image-bearers of the divine, should never be treated as objects or things that help enrich others. This is the "thing" oriented society that Dr. King condemned, which treats individuals as tools rather than reconciled sons and daughters of the same creator. King wrote that in order to usher in this new order of love and reconciliation, the thriving of the human must be more important than the luxuries of a few. He further argued that a civilization can become broken not merely through financial bankruptcy.

> *We must rapidly begin the shift from a "thing"-oriented society to a "person"-oriented society. When machines and computers, profit motives and property rights are considered more important than people, the giant triplets of racism, materialism and militarism are incapable of being conquered. A civilization can flounder as readily in the face of moral and spiritual bankruptcy as it can through financial bankruptcy (Ibid., 183).*

This fall of civilization that occurs through spiritual bankruptcy rather than financial bankruptcy is consistent with the eschatological song of the virgin Mary which says *the rich will be sent away empty.* The spiritual bankruptcy that follows greed and materialism leads to moral decline which impacts every sector of society: academic, political, cultural and economic.

In a predatory economy, the cost of goods and services is raised to the level where debt must be acquired to obtain them. Interest is charged on the loans which are given, which keeps the borrower enslaved to the lender. The reality that is overlooked is that the rich are oftentimes indebted to the poor due to unfair wages, yet the reverse is true. The predatory economies of this generation are debt-based economies because this allows the lender to control the borrower and further exploit and manipulate. Africa is the wealthiest continent in the world as it relates to mineral resources, yet those who pay monies to extract these minerals do not share the wealth with those who extracted them. When considering its mineral resources, and those who live in luxury because of them, no African country should in debt to any Western nation. Wealthy nations are indebted to Africa and should view themselves as such when making exchanges and engaging in trade with the continent. Africa should be one of the wealthiest continents in the world were it not for debt economies and exploitation of its mineral wealth. In order to achieve reconciliation surrounding the economic systems, thievery of Africa's resources through child labor and starvation wages must end. A just economy which seeks the advancement and progress of the human race must be firmly established in the world. The poor will be uplifted, and the rich will lose nothing in the process.

> *In this sense God's redeeming work transforms the economy of debt into the economy of grace. The appropriate prayer to be prayed in the economy of grace is, "Forgive us our debts as we forgive our debtors (Soulen and Woodhead 2006: 181)."*

Christian theologians based in western cultures should reconsider the ideas that Darwinian capitalism is a system of freedom and progress. Such are broken systems of enslavement, thievery and dehumanization. They should condemn the abuses within these systems as contrary to a reconciled new world order and morally bankrupt. Debts that are held against exploited populations should be immediately forgiven, and conversely those who have engaged in exploitation should consider their own indebtedness to the poorer nations. Neither should wealthy nations utilize debt to control the economies of the world. Those who are at the bottom of the economic ladder should be respected as equal to those at the top of the ladder and given their just due. Professor Dwight Hopkins explains how the biblical narratives are indicative of a God who stands shoulder-to-shoulder with the oppressed when they are victimized and manipulated by the powerful. He expounds on how God's inclination to stand up for the oppressed involves more than spiritual support but also socio-economic deliverance. Hopkins suggests that it is God's design that the majority world of non-white nations and people groups should have their rightful share of Earth's resources. He further suggests that is not the design of Jesus for the imperialistic and monopolistic minority dominate those resources.

> *And when they, the majority of the world, are able to practice spiritual and material freedom, then the minority groups who have a monopoly on most resources on earth will also have a chance to be free from their sin of keeping almost all of God's resources from themselves. Dominant theologies say they are universal. But they really wear a mask to hide the domination of the few over the many. Black theology of liberation states openly its leaning toward the majority of the world in order to work with the spirit of freedom for all. (Hopkins 1999: 23)*

Dominant theologies indeed focus on the needs of the world and even the problem of poverty but fail to focus on the political and structural reasons for much of the poverty that exists. Those dominant theologies also often fail to take notice on their own contributions to those systems of economic slavery, through their sins of omission and cultural pride. Hopkins is correct. The biblical stories do not stop at the need for spiritual liberation.

> *The biblical emancipation was not only feeing the invisible spirits of the slaves but also the freeing of real workers who were real slaves to the ruling class, whose purpose was the accumulation of profit based the forced and unjust labor of working, oppressed humanity (Ibid, 23).*

Moses, Ezekiel, Jeremiah, Zephaniah, Daniel and Amos proclaimed a theology aimed at destroying both the spiritual structures as well as dismantling unjust political and economic patterns which enabled greed and disabled those who sought freedom and liberation. Jesus was the chief among them. *The glue that holds together all the stories of the Bible is God siding with the poor for everyone's full humanity on earth. No amount of spiritualizing or metaphysical discourse...can erase the clear biblical story of God in Jesus in the poverty of a manger* (Ibid, 24). This political side of the coin cannot be excluded from the Jesus' view of reconciliation. Those churches and ecclesiastical institutions who are in close proximity with the most powerful have a responsibility to advance that political side of the equation for the freeing of sacred humanity and for the reconciliation work that Jesus began.

6.8 Reconciliation includes the demand justice without revenge or retaliation

Demands for justice are often mistaken for hatred, retribution, or retaliation on the part of the victim. Additionally, calls for justice are often mistakenly viewed as the antithesis forgiveness and love. Passionately advocating on behalf of the exploited and oppressed should not be confused with hatred towards the perpetrator. A Christological perspective would clearly show that love and justice go hand in hand. Christ condemned the Pharisees, scribes, and moneychangers for their abuses of the poor, desperate and unlearned, yet he loved fully and completely. Jesus of Nazareth advocated for the widows and fatherless, but his advocacy did not involve hatred and retaliation against those who were the causes of their pain. Christ both warned against retaliation (Matt. 5:38 KJV) and advocated for justice. In Christ's teachings on justice, he warned his generation that they were not in harmony with the spirit of the law which they claimed to uphold. The leaders and rulers of the Jews, according to Jesus had lost sight of the most important aspects of the law, which are justice (restoration of the victim and fair application of the law against abusers), mercy (compassion for the poor and needy) and faithfulness (honest interactions in business and religious transactions) (Matthew 23:23 KJV).

It is possible to avoid retaliation while seeking justice. Retaliation is the seeking to inflict pain and suffering upon the abuser, due to anger caused by the harm inflicted. Christ's warning against retaliation suggests that if a just settlement can be reached out of court, it should be agreed to by the victim (Matthew 5:25). Jesus taught that in rejecting a just settlement out of court due to revenge and retaliation, it could be that the compensation may not be received and that the abused may themselves be unjustly condemned. Justice does not require a trial in such a case, because the purpose is to receive due compensation and restoration. One should not murder someone's family member out of retaliation because a member of one's family has been murdered. Forgiveness in this case is choosing not to murder but allowing the legal process to unfold. It is possible that one can simultaneously love the murderer and seek the appropriate application of the law against the criminal. It is possible that the court systems can be used for revenge and retaliation under the cloak of seeking justice. This can occur through exaggeration of claims or pain inflicted in order to inflict a greater level of pain against the accused. However, it must be understood that forgiveness, love, justice, and righteousness are all linked together.

Revenge and retaliation, when it is rendered, does not repair nor restore; it simply brings temporary feelings of satisfaction. When revenge and retaliation are carried out, everyone loses in the process. The human dignity of the accused must be honored even by those who have been unjustly treated.

> *Forms of justice that seek revenge or retribution, even by legal means, fail to bring about the full restoration of human dignity, even though they may leave the victim "feeling better," recompensed or authenticated in the face of the enemy or the perpetrator (Soulen and Woodhead 2006: 50).*

When individuals, communities or nations suffer at the hands of powerful opponents, one must discipline the inner drive for retaliation from the rightful call for repair and compensation. These emotions are real, but they must be mastered for the good of the community in need of repair. In such cases of retaliation, observers may confuse the victim with the victimizer. Satisfying the urge for revenge, fails to satisfy the need for restoration and compensation which are desperately needed.

Archbishop Desmond Tutu explained to fellow South Africans that forgiveness is not surrendering to an undeserving enemy, but rather it is an act of self-preservation. He argued that retaliation and revenge is counterproductive to the good that the oppressed are seeking. He challenged the citizens of South Africa and oppressed people around the world to reexamine the implications of forgiveness.

> *To forgive is not just to be altruistic. It is the best form of self-interest. What dehumanizes you inexorably dehumanizes me. It gives people resilience, enabling them to survive and emerge still human despite all efforts to dehumanize them (Tutu 1999: 32).*

Christian theology teaches what Archbishop Tutu expresses, which is that to forgive is to be human. He agrees that forgiveness is choosing not to hate and seek revenge while simultaneously seeking true justice. Since forgiveness is a quality of being human, it also places retaliation where it belongs. It is the retaliation against the urge to dehumanize one's own humanity through the dehumanizing of another. Forgiveness draws a line in the sand and says, "I will not be dehumanized by hatred and bitterness, and I will continue to function and thrive in my humanity through love." Theological anthropology says that we are created in the image of God, and the New Testament additionally says *God is love* (1 John 4:9). To love is to rebel against what dehumanizes. Nelson Mandela struggled for freedom in South Africa. He was imprisoned for over 20 years because of his fight for freedom. While there he was tortured, deprived of necessities and dehumanized, but he too learned that to love is natural to human nature. He understood that hate is unnatural and therefore must be taught. Mandela stated the following in his autobiography, *Long Walk to Freedom*:

> *No one is born hating another person because of the colour of his skin, or his background, or his religion. People must learn to hate, and if they can learn to hate, they can be taught to love, for love comes more naturally to the human heart than its opposite (Mandela 1994: 542).*

Archbishop Desmond Tutu described the ability to forgive is to be able to survive being human in a world of cruelty, hatred and hostility. When the oppressor inflicts harm upon the weak, he is considered inhumane. When the oppressed lose their humanity and come down to the level of the oppressor through inhumanity, they dehumanize themselves by duplicating the actions of the inhumane. This explains why Tutu suggested that forgiveness is not merely altruistic but in the interest of oneself and community. Dr. Martin Luther King Jr agrees with Archbishop Tutu's view of forgiveness and humanity. King argued that hate, retaliation, and bitterness are self-defeating concepts and does nothing to advance the cause of the abuse. He suggested that these negative concepts are too high a price to pay as the lessons of history are considered.

> *We can no longer afford to worship the God of hate or bow before the altar of retaliation. The oceans of history are made turbulent by the ever-rising tides of hate. History is cluttered with the wreckage of nations and individuals who*

pursued this self-defeating path of hate (King 1967: 187).

It is often the case that societies where oppressed communities reside can misunderstand the call for justice as an expression of hatred and animosity. However, most oppressed communities desire freedom and repair more than retaliation. King saw this fear of retaliation as resulting from hidden guilt from communities who have won their privilege through marginalization. *A guilt-ridden white minority fears that if the Negro attains power, he will without restraint or pity act to revenge the accumulated injustices and brutality of the years* (Ibid., 69). This principle applies not only to racial relations in America, but among groups all over the world. Awareness of this guilt complex does not mean that it is the responsibility of the oppressed to assuage the fears of the oppressor concerning retaliation, but rather it means that the oppressor should listen more carefully to the cries for deliverance. Should the oppressor listen more carefully, they will find within those marginalized groups the same humanity they see in themselves. The privileged classes should come to terms with historical wrongs and acknowledge them. It is then that the guilt can be addressed. Additionally, addressing the guilt means understanding that both the oppressor and the oppressed are alike robbed wherever there is injustice. As Mandela stated, *A man who takes away another man's freedom is a prisoner of hatred, he is locked behind the doors of prejudice and narrow-mindedness. I am not truly free when I am taking away someone else's freedom. The oppressed and the oppressor are alike robbed of their humanity* (Mandela 1994: 544).

The ministry of reconciliation understands that all humanity shares a common enemy which dehumanizes, which is fear, greed and hatred. All have been robbed in a sense by these thieves of humanity. In combatting them together, the human race comes closer to taking hold of the God given freedom to love, to flourish and exist as one human family.

6.9 Fear is an unnecessary and irrational burden that alienates rather than reconciles.

It is the "fear of insignificance" that will keep the oppressor from taking on an attitude of humility and assuming the posture of a compassionate empathetic listener that reconciliation demands, but faith must be stronger than fear. Perfect love casts out fear of the other, fear of chaos, fear of the future and fear of insignificance and death. The fear that the privileged class will lose their superior status within their world is unwarranted. One's unique quality as a human should not depend on the deprivation and the dehumanization of another. Theological anthropology shows that all humans are unique and special based on the reality that they are creatures designed by God to glorify their maker in the fulfilment of their purpose. Depending upon societal privilege to give meaning to one's human existence misinterprets what it means to be human. Realizing what it means to be human, says that one's specialness and distinctiveness does not change when others are liberated and receive their just due. When the liberated receive equal treatment as humans, one should not fear that this will in any way diminishes his or her humanity. Dr. Martin Luther King referred to such fears as irrational. He further defined these emotions as fear of the loss of economic privilege, social status, change and adjustments. Another fear is that of interracial marriage, which King mentioned. King suggested that cruelty, violence and deception directed at those who struggle for liberation, are fruitless efforts to combat such fears. He adds that such efforts to combat change due to fear create more fear and greater psychological imprisonment in the process.

Instead of eliminating fear, they instill deeper and more pathological fears. The white man, through his own efforts, through education and goodwill, through searching his conscience and through confronting the fact of integration, must do a great deal to free himself of these paralyzing fears (King 1967: 68).

While King is specifically addressing a localized situation in the United States, the principles that he contributes can be applied in similar situations around the world wherever oppression exists. The same may apply in the Israeli and Palestinian conflict. Similar applications may be made in the Turkish and Kurdish situation. China and its persecution of ethnic and religious groups in its region, as well as and other conflict areas in the world should take heed. All may gain practical wisdom from these words. All societies in order to address collective guilt and fear by the privileged groups, must alike educate and scrutinize themselves in order to free themselves from their own psychological chains of fear. Roger Fisher and William Ury, referenced in an earlier chapter in this thesis, also address the roots of such fears,

> *People tend to assume that whatever they fear, the other side intends to do...It is all too easy to fall into the habit of putting the worst interpretation on what the other side says or does. A suspicious interpretation often follows naturally from one's existing perceptions (Ury and Fisher 1981: 19-22).*

True reconciliation requires faith in humanity which should cast out fear of each other. There is no need for Europeans to fear that the world will descend into chaos if Africans, Asians, and Arabs share power and equal stewardship of the world. There is no need to fear that other nations will seek deadly retribution upon the great powers should the rise in wealth and influence. William Ury and Roger Fisher detail the psychological fears of communities who hold such fears. What stands out in Ury, and Fisher's analysis is the idea of communities viewing the world from their own background and experience instead of the vantage point of their human neighbors. They write about the reinforced prejudices and imaginary interpretations that occur when egos are threatened.

> *They have egos that are easily threatened. They see the world from their own personal vantage point, and they frequently confuse their perceptions with reality. Routinely, they fail to interpret what you say in the way you intend...Misunderstanding can reinforce prejudice and lead to reactions that produce counterreactions in a vicious circle... (Ibid., 14).*

There is no need to fear that Europeans and White America will be humiliated and disrespected because they confess their past wrongs and show equal respect to other less developed nations. There is no need to fear the differences of other cultures that may dilute the uniqueness of one's own culture. There is no need to fear a future where familyhood, togetherness and love for humanity are the highest values. There is no need to fear a lack of resources, for as the freer the world becomes the more creativity, ingenuity and resourcefulness will emerge.

The fear of appearing weak because one has chosen to stand aside and listen, compromise, or acknowledge past wrongs is unfounded. American culture and theology suggest that compromise and showing respect for enemies demonstrates weakness and emboldens enemies. It is thought that giving recognition through dialogue with enemies opens the door for attacks. However, what is true is that the one who is willing to compromise and acknowledge past wrongs is the strongest, because they have no fears of being diminished simply because they behave like humans with compassion. They do not need to threaten or intimidate in order to show strength; their strength is not merely found in the threat war, but strength of character. Compromise and confession do not invite violence but create an atmosphere of mutual respect and equal humanity. What ends the cycle of violence, or the threat of violence is when justice mingled with compassion.

> *How can we end the cycle of violence? For Father Ateek the answer to that question is justice, but more than justice. It is a justice tempered by mercy and forgiveness. We must learn to love, not just our neighbors, but our enemies. This does not mean accepting injustice from them. But it does mean trying to understand their hurts, the story behind their fears and their need to dominate...This is the ethic and spirituality called compassion (Ateek 2014: 6).*

Reconciliation and beloved community cannot be accomplished without intentional movements commitments toward justice. In order to achieve justice, there must be first an acknowledgment of wrongdoing. Furthermore, justice is always restorative and not merely promises of future good. Simultaneously, there must be efforts by the oppressed to understand the fears of those within the dominant society. This does not mean accepting the wrong or excusing it, but listening is a part of extending respect and dignity.

According to black and womanist theologian, Kelly Brown Douglas, true reconciliation involves more than sympathy or even solidarity: She eloquently states what is required, which actively seeks to eradicate all that stands in the way of human dignity:

> *[It requires] a steadfast commitment to doing the work that will carry on well beyond the protest to overcome 'a white way of knowing' that stands in the way of any notion of Black equality...It is in recognizing that work is indicative of God's salvation. In this instance, it is the work that joins with God in redeeming the world from the original sin that 'raced' God's people into those who deserve life and those who do not (Douglas 2021: 205).*

One of the problems that stands in the way of that reconciliation is that arrogance that seeks to absolve itself of his terrible history, by pointing out all the good that has been done. One of the slogans of the religious right in America is *"We will never apologize for America."* It is this idea that "Christian" America has done so much good in the world, that it deserves to be congratulated and not condemned, that stands in the way. Failure to admit wrongdoing and refusal to engage in dialogue is not a sign of strength but a sign of self-defeating irrationality. One's love for humanity should be greater than the fear of appearing weak or suffering embarrassment. This should especially be the case with clergy persons who embrace the Christological and eschatological mission of Christ.

The Pauline discourse eloquently explained Christ's relationship to the human race who were once seen as his enemies. The apostle said, *our friendship with God was restored by the death of his Son while we were still his enemies...* (Romans 5:10). Christ was not concerned with appearing weak, soft, provocative, or losing prestige through the condescension evident in the incarnation on behalf of his enemies.

> *Who, being in very nature God, did not consider equality with God something to be used to his own advantage;*

Instead, he gave up his divine privileges; he took the humble position of a slave and was born as a human being. When he appeared in human form, he humbled himself in obedience to God and died a criminal's death on a cross (Philippians 2:6-9, New Living Translation).

Although Jesus was divine, he was not concerned about embarrassment or shame in his work to fulfill his purpose on behalf of his enemies. He was willing to place himself on the same level as a human as his enemies were and to be viewed as a criminal. Suffering the death of the cross, was the extent he was willing to go in order to reconcile his enemies. Rather than diminishing him, it caused him to be exalted. Having humbled himself in this way, he consequently became exalted above all principalities and powers.

Any Christian society, which are among the most powerful in the world, should embrace this humble approach in order to bring healing and reconciliation among the nations. Shame and ridicule are risks worthy of taking for the sake of the salvation of human relationships and the peaceful survival of the race. The humiliation that one may endure is worth experiencing in order to break the chains of alienation, marginalization oppression and exploitation. The flourishing and the advancement of the human race will be found worthy of the assumed diminishment of societal prestige. Humanity is one family, and none are complete until are complete. When one part of the family is hurting, the entire family suffers. The human family rises and falls together. It is the work of Christ through his followers to lift all that are broken and left behind, so that humanity can become one united family bringing glory to the creator and fulfilling the divine purposes. This will usher in an era of a more natural, harmonious, and joyful and loving co-existence for the entire race where all populations may together function in their God given dignity which the creator intended. Alex Walker agrees with this anthropological view of the full and free functioning of the human race. She writes how dehumanization can never bring happiness as it prevents the dehumanizer from operating within their higher instincts. Violence, conflict and oppression will be greatly lessened when all the human family concludes that we all belong together on Earth with our freedom and dignity intact.

> *...We do, in fact, belong here, and have a right to be here, unmolested and protected in our homes, churches, mosques, and schools. We are designed, I believe, as human beings, to instinctively wish to protect and cherish each other. We must be taught—those who are not born sociopathic—how to be stonily merciful (Makdisi 2010: 22).*

This movement of reconciling with one's own humanity and being reconciled with the humanity of others must be untiring work of Christian theologians, Christian leaders, ecclesiastical organizations, denominations, non-profits, corporations, politicians, and clergy who lovingly desire to fulfill the designs of Christ. It is then that we may harmonize with our best instincts with which the Creator originally designed the human race and together function in the enjoyment and happiness which divinity intended. When Christian theologians and clergypersons understand that the waters of baptism with its vision of new life runs deeper than the blood of nationalism and racial fears, the world will know what reconciliation truly means. However, such theology must move from theories to actual problem solving and reconciling practices that liberates and creates familyhood among the masses on planet earth.

6.10 Study and Implementation of Reconciling Practices is Urgently Needed.

That form of reconciliation that is consistent with the gospel of Jesus, when it comes to societal reconciliation, according to Professor Terrence Tilley, requires much more than that of personal forgiveness. Personal reconciliation involves restoring a particular broken relationship, but societal reconciliation involves rebuilding what Tilley describes as the "moral order of a society." This social reconciliation involves much more than increased dialogue, respect, and togetherness, it involves taking political action to transform governments in ways which lifts the downtrodden and allows them to function in accordance with the

Maker's designs. He adds that promises of a just society must be conducted in a way that avoids revenge, punishment, and retribution. He reminds his readers, that such political action cannot be conducted in a haphazard way, but with reverence and due diligence. He adds that it cannot simply be the activity of the most prominent advocates, but as a mark of true citizenship and civic responsibility. Tilley outlines some of the practical and political areas by which social reconciliation may be accomplished. Tilley proposes the following practical directions for social reconciliation:

> *The better path, one beyond revenge and 'rebalancing,' toward reconciliation, remembers fallen victims, recognizes victimized and victimizing victims, and provides ways to redress, at least in part, the tragic effects of past evils, The goal is not 'rebalancing' but the creation of a future together that stands a real chance of not replicating the past (Tilley 2008: 208).*

Tilley rightly reminds the community of faith that reconciliation is not the end goal, but the prerequisite for serving the creator's purpose with a sense of togetherness. Reconciliation helps the community by helping them the value of each other's gifts and learning how to benefit from them. It is upon this basis that much good can be achieved.

Next, Professor Tilley suggests the need of reconciling actions that lead to a vibrant health care system that does not discriminate against nor bankrupts the poor. Just as Jesus came to demonstrate God's desire to see suffering humanity experience physical healing and not just on a spiritual level. Part of this healing dynamic, according to Tilley, is the reconciling action of ensuring clean water for the most vulnerable population groups. Such a healing paradigm is consistent with the good news of Jesus. Poisoned water in low-income populations will be unimaginable in a world that embraces the healing gospel. It does not guarantee clean water for the higher classes while ignoring that which sickens the poor. These reconciling actions does not merely place the burden on individuals but upon the political structures as well (Ibid., 294).

Tilley further suggests that reconciling practices must require of its citizenry a righteous political structure that will facilitate the acquisition of food, clothing, shelter, medicine for all, regardless of their background or social status. Such practices, according to Tilley presses toward a world where the disabled, the widow and those who have been cut off from employment will not suffer due to events not under their control (Ibid., 295). This reconciliation imagines a world where such safety nets are not considered as shameful hand-outs, but a Christ-like reflection of a society's appreciation of the image of God which is present in "the least of these."

Finally, Tilley envisioned "social reconciliation" as necessary for the purpose of engaging in a righteous social "reconstruction." In his view, reconciliation happens at the conclusion of any conflict and war, but its aftermath must build upon this reconciliation through a new age of reconstruction of a "moral order of society." He adds that this reconstruction must reshape its laws in a more just and equitable manner allowing the voices of all to be heard. This reconstruction that follows reconciliation, according to Tilley, must encourage "avenues of reparation," not to punish the powerful, but to rightfully support victims in their recovery loses endured due to abusive structures." He states conclusively the following.

> *While societies differ in many ways—and the global society is even more complex—such reconciliation requires a strengthening of law, a democratic and verifiable process, so as to make possible the participation of all, and avenues of reparation not for the sake of vengeance but so that victims can recover 'at least some measure of what they have lost...' (Tilley 2008: 290)*

Tilley's ideas of practical reconciliation should be carefully analyzed and implemented. They represent Jesus' vision for the world. Tilley is correct when he suggests that individual reconciliation is important, but reconciliation and reconstruction of broken societies through political action does indeed fulfill the work of Jesus. The ideas of reconciliation and reconstruction of

Professor Tilley are supported by Christian author, Jemar Tisby. Tisby encourages Christian leaders not to wait for the oppressed to voice their concerns but to take action to study whether there have been problems in the past that need to be addressed. He suggests that religious institutions and other institutions should take the initiative and study their organizational past. He acknowledges that this is a challenging task, but such actions cannot be ignored. Failure to study one's own history, will undermine future efforts for human rights advocacy. One hopeful area in the academic arena may be seen in the Universities Studying Slavery group, which explores the history of discriminatory actions and histories of White supremacy within the university realm (Tisby 2021:89). Such studies revisit not only potential involvement in Slavery by universities, but the history of declining the applications of potential students since they were black.

The reconciling actions that need to be taken are numerous, but such reconciling practices cannot exclude the following:

1. End dehumanizing stereotypes of Africa, The Middle East and Asia in the global media as the face of poverty, chaos and helplessness

2. End white supremacy through dismantling systems which privilege certain sectors of society and also through re-education concerning the great contributions of black civilizations in history

3. White preachers, clergypersons and theologians must frequently preach and teach against white supremacy as a horrific sin against the Creator without deflection, excuse or what-about-ism.

4. End the military and prison industrial complex

5. End forced child labor and sweat shops as means driving the global economy. Create humane ways to drive down costs and pricing without burdening and enslaving the most

vulnerable

6. End the objectification of women as an economic catalyst

7. Re-empower Africa to utilize and fully develop their own natural resources for the exportation of finished goods and products rather than exploit its mineral resources and raw materials such as cell phones, tablets, and computers

8. Denuclearize the powerful nations and work together for the survival and flourishing of the human race through acting against climate change

9. Demilitarize the police forces and move toward respecting the dignity of the masses rather than viewing them as suspects or enemies

10. Proclaim human rights in national and international spheres (Tilley 2008: 289)

11. Promote, invest and facilitate educational opportunities for young girls and the poor.

12. Respect the dignity, sovereignty, self-determination and territorial integrity of Latin America, the Middle East and Africa

13. Introduce public apologies for historical human rights abuses by governments and corporations. Ecclesiastical organizations must introduce seasons of public confession and lament within their organizations and denominations. Include such expressions of lament in liturgical readings as Professor Terrance Tilley suggested. Seek active and tangible gestures of atonement within communities who have been wronged.

14. Introduce the study of historic economic theft and work for the implementation of economic reparation. This includes the restoration of stolen indigenous lands.

15. Former colonial powers must release their former colonies

from unjust debts.

16. Work together to end human trafficking and modern slavery

17. End the occupation, demonization, and strategic displacement of the Palestinians. Return to the 1967 borders for Israel and Palestine and divide Jerusalem between East and West among the two parties.

18. End the destruction and logging of rainforests not only for ecological and environmental reasons but also to protect indigenous people, lands, cultures, and lifestyles.

This New Testament concept of reconciliation was also advanced by New Testament theologian and New York Times columnist, Professor Esau McCaulley of Wheaton College. McCaulley eloquently describes Jesus' eschatological vision for reconciliation in his book, *Reading While Black*. McCaulley notes that just as the original creation of God is the ideal that must be the standard all must work toward, this is also true concerning the future eschatological vision. Whatever is God's vision for the future world is the eternal standard for all times, and believers should serve that end.

> *What is God's vision for the reconciliation of all things (Rev 21: 3-4)? It is a community of the healed and transformed, not the enslaved. If Christian ethics is about living now in light of the coming future, then the coming future freedom of all people has to at some point become flesh in the formerly enslaved bodies whose very physical freedom is an enacted parable of the gospel (McCaulley 2020: 145).*

Professor McCaulley also emphasized that the spirit of togetherness must not require that diverse people groups assimilate into the dominant cultures of the world. He explained that reconciliation demands that all cultures will be celebrated and embraced in that spirit of reconciliation. Forced assimilation is not reconciliation but oppression. McCaulley points out how all tribes, cultures and nations remain intact in John's future vision. Reconciliation, therefore, must never demand assimilation, but embrace other ethnic identities. Reconciliation means that there must be a society where all are comfortable, no matter where they reside, functioning in the uniqueness of their culture. In John's vision, no one is ashamed of the color of their skin due to the dominant culture's brainwashing, but thankful for their God-given beauty and dignity. Remember that John saw the diversity of the people, which means he saw the variety of skin complexions in the future world standing in their pride and dignity. McCaulley further suggests that to be ashamed of one's skin color by centering or normalizing Western ideas of beauty and dignity limits the gifts of God within us all. Christ empowered reconciliation never sanctions the diminishing of one's ethnic identity in order to achieve oneness and familyhood. Reconciliation embraces the beauty and contribution of all. Notice the words of the professor concerning John's vision of multiethnic community in the following:

> *Each in its own way highlights diversity...At the end, we do not find the elimination of difference. Instead, the very diversity of cultures is a manifestation of God's glory. God's eschatological vision for the reconciliation of all things in his Son requires my blackness and my neighbors' Latina identity to endure forever. Colorblindness is sub-biblical and falls short of the glory of God...Therefore inasmuch as I modulate my blackness or neglect my culture, I am placing limits on the gifts God has given me to offer to his church and kingdom (Ibid., 119).*

Reconciliation calls for unity but never uniformity. Theologian Claude Atcho eloquently expressed this idea when he said that reconciliation *makes sense only when ethnic difference is not erased by the* gospel (Atcho 2022: 168). He further adds that Paul's view of reconciliation is *not the obliteration of difference but rather the obliteration of dominance (Ibid., 168)*. This reconciliation enjoys and celebrates the dignity of each aspect of the multiethnic community. Loving one's neighbor means respecting their unique perspectives, experiences and contributions and not requiring them to change or modulate who they are in order to be fully embraced. To do so, according to McCaulley is to disrespect the unique qualities of a communities given by the Creator. Atcho defines the link between loving our own ethic people and the broader multiethnic community within the context of reconciliation. Atcho interprets Paul's love for his own kin, which he never relinquished in order to love in an expansive way the Gentiles, which he expressed in Romans 9. He utilizes Paul's words in order to provide a template for those who love and struggle for their own kin, while embracing the larger family of humanity. In Romans 9, Paul expressed his love and desire for Israel as his nation and kin, but this did not prevent him from loving the Gentiles who were not his kin "according to the flesh." Atcho notes that Paul also respected the cultural identity of non-Jews, not requiring or expecting them to be circumcised in order to be included. Atcho refers to the New Testament concept that refers to those who were not "my people" now becoming his people through Jesus. He points out that this does not cause his love for his first people to die away.

> *Those who were not our people become our people through spiritual union, by being bound up together with Jesus...the love for our first people does not die...As the apostle to the Gentiles [Paul], he longed for his people (Israel) and welcomed those people (Gentiles) in a way that melded them into one new longing patterned after God's expansive love in Jesus...This means that, in Jesus, we gain a new diverse people without the obliteration of our ethnic identity...(Atcho 2020: 169).*

Oftentimes without proper contemplation, Anglo society, by centering themselves, make others uncomfortable in their difference and unwittingly show that they are uncomfortable with difference. They often take offense when marginalized communities assert their humanity and take pride in their culture as a psychological reaction to racism and struggles with inferiority complexes. Many unwittingly desire that such pride and love of kin be relinquished, and that colorblindness be the standard of love. Historically disenfranchised communities should not be required to change their cultural names, lingo, dress, worship styles, education, rhythm, dance, music, or family values in order to be viewed as reconciled. Loving your neighbor, in the context of reconciliation means empathizing with the struggle of cultures who have historically been discriminated against and their battle against the psychological warfare they have experienced in their history. Loving your neighbor includes loving their difference and not requiring them to relinquish their identity and culture to be included. This has been one of the failures of missionary societies and Anglo-American Ecclesiastical bodies.

Additionally, loving one's neighbor, means more than showing kindnesses, shaking hands, not spewing slurs or physical embrace, but it means hating anything that will rob one of the diverse people groups of the dignity they deserve. Loving one's neighbor, in the context of reconciliation means working against anything that will enslave, reduce to poverty, or discriminate against another ethnic community due to ignorance or prejudice. Loving your neighbor means seeing your own children in the faces of the children of other races and nationalities. This love means that one will appreciate when others who have been historically vilified have learned how to love themselves. This love will not be offended when one demonstrates love toward their own due to being historically unloved. This self-love will not be offensive to the dominant groups who once hated them, but it will be applauded. This is the vision of reconciliation. Reconciliation and love of neighbor means working against all things that destroy their communities due to war or environmental factors. It means listening to the cries of the oppressed rather than operating in pride and self-justification. This work is not an easy one, but bearing the cross involves doing what is not necessarily easy. It is my prayer that the community of faith will commit themselves to this work of reconciliation, reconstruction and repair to the glory and honor of Jesus of Nazareth.

Dr. Eric Betts

BIBLIOGRAPHY

Amar-Dahl, Tamar. (2016). *Zionist Israel and the Question of Palestine*, /Berlin, Free University.

Araujo, Ana Lucia. (2017). *Reparations for Slavery and the Slave Trade,* New York: Bloomsbury Publishing

Arnold, Glen., (1977). Interview with Jesse Jackson: You Can Pray If You Want To | Christianity Today

Atcho, Claude. (2022). *Reading Black Books*. Grand Rapids MI: Brazos Press

Ateek, Naim Stephan., (2008). *A Palestinian Christian Cry for Reconciliation.* Maryknoll, NY: Orbis Publications

Ateek, Naim Stephan., (2014). *Justice and Justice Only.* Maryknoll, NY: Orbis Publications

Ateek, Naim Stephan., (2017). *A Palestinian Theology of Liberation.* Maryknoll, NY: Orbis Publications

Battle, Michael., (2009). *Ubuntu: I in You and You in Me*. New York: Seabury Books

Battle, Michael., (2017) *Heaven on Earth: God's Call to Community in the Book of Revelation.* Louisville, Kentucky: Westminster John Knox Press.

Bible, *King James Version*

Buckingham, Marcus. (2005). *The One Thing You Need to Know*. New York: Free Press.

Carl, Nicole., and Ravitch, Sharon., (2019). *Qualitative Research: Bridging the Conceptual, Theoretical, and Methodological, Edition 2.* Thousand Oaks CA: Sage Publications

Carter, Jimmy. (2006). *Palestine Peace Not Apartheid*. New York: Simon and Shuster

Cook, Susan (2004). *Genocide in Rwanda and Cambodia*. New Brunswick, NJ: Transaction Publishers

Cone, James, H. (2018). *Black Theology and Black Power*. New York: Orbis Books.

Cone, James, H (1997). *The God of the Oppressed*. Maryknoll New York: Orbis Books

Cosby, Kevin (2021). *Getting to the Promised Land.* Westminster. John Knox Press

De Gruchy, John W. (2002). *Reconciliation: Restoring Justice*. Minneapolis: Fortress Press

Douglas, Kelly Brown. (2012). *Resurrection Hope: A Future Where Black Lives Matter*. New York: Orbis Books

Du Mez, Kristin. (2020) *Jesus and John Wayne: How White Evangelicals Corrupted a Faith and Fractured a Nation*. New York: Liveright Publishing.

Fernandez-Alban, Ary (2018) *Decolonizing Theology in Revolution.* Nashville, TN: Palgrave Macmillan.

Fisanick, C. (2004). *The Rwanda Genocide.* Farmington Hills, MI: Greenhaven Press.

Fischbach, Michael R. (2019). *Black Power and Palestine— Transnational Countries of Color.* Stanford, California: Standford University Press.

Fisher, R., Ury, W. (1981). *Getting to Yes, Negotiating Without Giving In*. New York: Penguin Publishing.

Flick, Uwe. (2018). *An Introduction to Qualitative Research*. Thousand Oaks, CA: Sage Publications.

Friedman, E. (2007). *Failure of Nerve*. New York: Church

Publishing.

Hagee, John., (2010). *Will America Survive?* Milan, TN: Simon and Shuster

Hopkins, Dwight., (1999). *Black Theology of Liberation.* Maryknoll, NY: Orbis Books.

Holy Bible: Holman Christian Standard Version. (2009). Nashville: Holman Bible Publishers.

Jones, Robert P., (2020) *White Too Long,* New York: Simon and Shuster Publishing

Kagan, Robert, (2017) *Backing into World War III.* Brookings Institute Available at *https://www.brookings.edu/research/backing-into-world-war-iii* Accessed 2020/05/19

Katongole, Emmanuel, (2009). *Mirror to the Church, Resurrecting Faith after Genocide in Rwanda.* Grand Rapids, MI: Zondervan

Katongole, Emmanel, (2011). *The Sacrifice of Africa—A Political Theology for Africa.* Grand Rapids Michigan: Wm. B. Eerdmans Publishing Company

King, Martin Luther Jr., (1967). *Where Do We Go from Here: Chaos or Community*, Boston: Beacon Press

King, Martin Luther Jr., (2013). *The Essential Martin Luther King Jr., "I Have a Dream" and Other Great Writings,* Boston: Beacon Press

Kwon, Duke L. and Gregory Thompson. (2021). *Reparations: A Christian Call for Reparations and Repair*, Grand Rapids MI: Brazos Press

Makdisi, Saree., (2010). *Palestine Inside Out—An Everday Occupation*, New York: W.W. Norton and Company

Mandela, Nelson., (1994). *Long Walk to Freedom.* London: Little, Brown and Company.

Mason, Eric., (2021). *Urban Apologetics: Restoring Black Dignity with the Gospel*: Grand Rapids, Michigan: Zondervan

McCauley, Esau., (2020) *Reading While Black*: Westmont, Illinois: Intervarsity Press

Milwood, Robinson A., *African Humanity*: (2012). A Sociological, Theological and Psychological Study, United Kingdom, Xlibris Corporation.

Miroslav, Volf., *Exclusion and Embrace*, Revised and Updated: (2019). Nashville TN: Abingdon Press

Morrissey, Christopher A., (2018). *Christianity and American State Violence in Iraq: Priestly or Prophetic?* Abingdon OX: Routledge

Munayer, Salim j. and Lisa Loden., (2012). *Land Cries Out*: Eugene Oregon: Wipfi and Stack Publishing

Nasserden, Les., (2019). *Debunking Christian Zionism and Evolutionary Creation*: Bloomington, IN: Westbow Press

Prior, Michael., (1999). Zionism and the State of Israel: A Moral Inquiry. London and New York, Routledge

Prior, Michael., (1997). *The Bible and Colonialism.* Sheffield England, Sheffield Academic Press

Rabeb, Mitri and Suzanne Henderson., (2017). *The Cross in Contexts, Suffering and Redemption in Palestine.* Mary Knoll, NY, Orbis Books

Raheb, Mitri, (2014). *Faith in the Face of an Empire.* Mary Knoll, NY, Orbis Books

Rainey, Brian., (2018). *Race, Ethnicity and Xenophobia in the Bible.* Abington England, Routledge

Roberts, J. Deotis, (1994). *Liberation and Reconciliation*, Mary Knoll, NY, Orbis Books

Ryrie, Charles., (1999). *Basic Theology*: Chicago Illinois, Moody Publishers

Samy, Shahira., (2010). *Reparations for Palestinian Refugees*: Abingdon, OX, Routledge

Schwarz, Tanya., (2016). *Ethiopian Jewish Immigrants*. New York. Routledge

Shalhoub-Kevorkian, Nadera., (2015). *Security Theology, Surveillance and the Politics of Fear.* Cambridge, United Kingdom: Cambridge University Press.

Smith, James H., (2022). *The Eyes of the World.* Chicago Illinois: University of Chicago Press.

Spector, Stephen., (2008). *Evangelicals and Israel*: Oxford England, Oxford University Press

Soulen, R. Kendall and Linda Woodhead., (2006). *God and Human Dignity,* Cambridge: William B. Eerdmans Publishing Company

Straus, Scott., (2006). *The Order of Genocide*. London: Cornell University Press.

The Holy Bible. (2015) New Living Translation. Carol Stream IL: Tyndale House Publishers.

Thurman, Howard., (1976) *Jesus and the Disinherited.* Boston Mass: Beacon Press.

Tilley, Terrance., (2008). *The Disciples' Jesus.* Maryknoll NY; Orbis Books.

Tutu, Desmond., (1999). *No Future without Forgiveness*. New York: Doubleday

Tisby, Jemar., (2021). *How to Fight Racism,* Grand Rapids, Michigan: Zondervan.

Mae Elise Cannon and Bruce N. Fisk, (2018) *Christian*

Nationalism and Christian Zionism: https://christiansforsocialaction.org/resource/christian-nationalism-and-christian-zionism-two-sides-of-the-same-coin/

Vaughn, Jasper, (2018) https://sojo.net/articles/how-some-american-evangelicals-are-challenging-views-about-palestine

Vogel, Christopher N. (2021) *Conflict Minerals Inc. War, Profit and White Saviorism in Eastern Congo.* New York: Oxford University Press.

Wang, Hansi Lo, (2021) *Why Black Lives Matter Supports the Pro-Palestinian Movemen*t: NPR

Willimon, William H. (2016). *Fear of the Other: No Fear in Love.* Nashville, TN: Abingdon Press

Younan, Munib., (2007). *An Ethical Critique of Christian Zionism, Journal of Lutheran Ethics,* Accessed May 15, 2020, http://ecla.org/JLE/Articles/509

SERMONS AND LECTURES

King, Martin Luther Jr., (June 1968). *The Drum Major Instinct.* (Sermon delivered at Ebenezer Baptist Church in Atlanta.) Retrieved from https://youtu.be/tBiFnDuCJIU

King, Martin Luther Jr., (October 15, 1962). *Symphony of Brotherhood. (Speech at Cornell College, Mt. Vernon, Ohio.)* Retrieved from https://youtu.be/bNPpEQkep2k

King, Martin Luther Jr., (Nov. 1957). *Loving Your Enemy.* (Sermon delivered at Dexter Avenue Church. Montgomery Alabama.) Retrieved from https://youtu.be/522wcqUlS0Y

Transcript: Jeremiah Wright's 9/11 Sermon | Otherwise Thinking (johnsmcclure.com) *Transcript: Jeremiah Wright's 9/11 Sermon | Otherwise Thinking (johnsmcclure.com)*

Robert Morris' sermon on Racism, https://www.christianpost.com/news/gateway-church-pastor-robert-morris-blames-americas-racism-on-ignorant-white-people.html

https://www.theosthinktank.co.uk/comment/2020/08/12/black-theology-an-introduction

Reddie, Anthony, Black theology: an introduction - Theos Think Tank - Understanding faith. Enriching society.

Use of secondary data in research - Online Tesis (online-tesis.com)

Sarr, Lucie, First African woman ever named to International Theological Commission (la-croix.com)

Moore, Charles Pulliam, UN Committee condemns U.S. for racial disparity, police brutality | PBS NewsHour

Domenica Ghanem, Be Very Afraid: Israeli Forces Are Training American Police (mintpressnews.com)

Gregory, Joel, Please listen to my friend Ralph West about racism and the SBC – Baptist News Global

Dr. Eric Betts

www.ingramcontent.com/pod-product-compliance
Lightning Source LLC
Chambersburg PA
CBHW072003110526
44592CB00012B/1185